Do Well by Doing Good

The Complete Guide to Charitable Remainder Trusts

Keith E. Gregg

Bonus Books, Inc., Chicago

00   99   98   5   4

Library of Congress Cataloging-in-Publication Data

Gregg, Keith E.
     Do well by doing good: the complete guide to charitable remainder
trusts/Keith E. Gregg.
          p.   cm.
     Includes index.
     ISBN 1–56625–068–4 (hardcover)
     1. Charitable uses, trusts, and foundations—United States—Marketing.
     I. Title
KF740.Z9G74   1996
361.7'4'0688—dc20   96–24649

Bonus Books, Inc.
160 East Illinois Street
Chicago, Illinois 60611

Composition by Point West, Inc., Carol Stream, Illinois
Printed in the United States of America

To my wife Catherine and son Robert for their love, patience and support. They have lived and witnessed what started out as a dream, became a goal, and is now a reality.

Contents

Contents

Author's Notes

This book is somewhat an act of frustration — frustrated by the fact that nothing really existed to show financial professionals, fund-raising executives and philanthropists the marketing side of the Charitable Remainder Trust.

There is a tremendous amount of technical information on the CRT, and blueprints on how the CRT works, but little if any information that shares the real life application and intrinsic value that this planned giving technique possesses.

For many years I have talked to people about the features and benefits of the Charitable Remainder Trust. Without having the tools to illustrate its potential, however, it is often like telling someone how to tie a shoe without having shoelaces to show them.

My intention with the creation of this book is to provide the complete guide for marketing the Charitable Remainder Trust, the diversity of the markets that exist, and those who can truly benefit from the CRT.

I hope this book conveys to you the benefits of doing well by doing good in such a way that it would have made Dale Carnegie proud. To paraphrase Carnegie, it's not so much what you say, it's how you say it that makes a world of difference in how well you market yourself or your services.

Do Well by Doing Good will teach you the finer points in marketing the CRT and how to say all the right things to the right audience. It will help identify donors that, until now, may have been inaccessible.

Do Well by Doing Good will afford you the opportunity to share the power of the Charitable Remainder Trust with corporations, foundations, associations and affluent individuals who might not otherwise want to visit with you until you've revealed to them the marvels of the CRT.

It truly is marvelous when you can couple economic benefit with philanthropy, and now we can help all those involved become winners — the donor, the charity and you as the planned giving professional.

Very seldom does everybody win, which is another reason the CRT is so special. If you as a donor are concerned about disinheriting heirs, don't be. We will discuss the Wealth Replacement Trust, which replaces those gifted assets, income and estate to heirs tax-free and we will show how we're able to maximize the gifts to multiple parties.

There is a true social value behind the Charitable Remainder Trust. With less government subsidy than ever before, the more than one million estimated charitable organizations in this country are in jeopardy. Unless there is a major focus on planned gifts, better than 50% of those organizations will no longer exist by the year 2010.

It is highly unlikely that people will give a large portion of their assets or estate if they feel it will jeopardize their own financial well being. But rather than hurt one's financial status, the CRT can enhance it. I believe, if conveyed to the potential donor in a way that emotionally moves them to give to a social cause or charity of their choice, they will.

One of the most important ways to accomplish this is to educate potential donors on the preservation or redirecting of their social capital. Renaissance, the country's largest CRT administrator, does a great job in spreading the message of social capital.

There are only two types of capital — *personal financial* is what we spend, save and live on. Then there's *social capital*, which is what we pay in the form of taxes. Through taxes, the government decides where to spend your money, whether it's on federal penitentiaries or social welfare programs. Either way, you don't control where that money goes. Now, the question is, if given the choice to redirect your social capital to your favorite charity, church, social cause or family foundation, would you?

The Charitable Remainder Trust enables you to do so and, in effect, may be the key to the survival and success of worthy charities.

If you ever wondered why more of this hasn't gone on if the Charitable Remainder Trust is such an appealing opportunity, I think it's because most people are uncomfortable talking about anything they aren't well versed in.

Doing Well by Doing Good is easy to read, easy to understand, and puts it in plain English. The power of the Charitable Remainder Trust lies in the marketing of this advanced gifting technique to those who can benefit the most.

When you do good for others,
you will do well for thy own self.

— Keith E. Gregg

Acknowledgments

Elton Brooks
Chairman
Renaissance, Inc.

...for educating me on the concept of social capital and how to re-direct it to serve the worthy causes of our choice.

Bob DiBella
National Sales Manager
PaineWebber

...for allowing me the opportunity to educate his brokers on the powerful uses of the Charitable Remainder Trust and, in turn, educating me on the many financial professionals' hunger for information and knowledge on how to market the CRT. This is what compelled me to deliver the first real-life, hands-on guide to marketing the Charitable Remainder Trust.

Jerry Huddleston
Vice President of Development
Boca Raton Community Hospital

...for reaffirming to me that even the most resourceful and affluent communities are in need of help in educating donors and creating long-term, successful and sustainable planned giving programs.

Bill Robinson
Senior Vice President
Pacific Mutual Life Insurance Company

...for having the foresight and vision to anticipate the financial services community's migration toward marketing to the affluent with advanced estate and planned giving techniques; and affording me the opportunity to speak, train and educate thousands of financial professionals to the enormous marketing opportunities that exist with the Charitable Remainder Trust.

Dr. Jimmy Calloway
Vice President
Government Affairs and Fund Development
Organization Committee
1996 Atlanta Paralympics

...for allowing me the opportunity to represent this remarkable organization in educating business leaders, corporations, associations and individuals on how they can "do well by doing good" and help worthy causes such as the Paralympics and the American Disabled Athletes Fund.

National Society of Fund Raising Executives (NSFRE)

...for the association's work in educating, promoting and facilitating the needs of so many wonderful charities and their causes; and for preparing me to be a messenger to tell the world that we can all make a difference.

Jim and Jean McLean
Philanthropists

...for opening my eyes through their gratitude and appreciation in sharing the joys of the Charitable Remainder Trust; and for the graciousness that created two more philanthropists in the world.

Introduction

The very title of this book, *Do Well by Doing Good*, defines both the essence of a Charitable Remainder Trust (CRT) and the intrinsic philosophy of those most likely to identify with its rewards. With a CRT, doing well and doing good are made easier. But until now there has been no definitive guide on how to market and make sense of this sophisticated form of deferred charitable giving.

Do Well by Doing Good strips away the complexities surrounding CRTs to reveal a double pay-off that is rather simple; while investing in a charity closest to their heart, donors benefit from a tax-exempt trust that provides them a lifetime of income.

In partnering an investment strategy with a charitable organization, CRTs have in turn coupled philanthropy and economic benefit, a novel concept that may prove the wave of the future.

The 1969 Tax Act created the Charitable Remainder Trust with this union in mind, but only in recent years have

CRTs gained prominence among other Planned Giving Arrangements. Investors realizing the dramatic shift in this country's financial resources have looked to CRTs as a powerful tool in securing both their personal and financial goals.

In the next 10 years, $1.5 trillion is expected to pass from one generation of Americans to the next, the largest transfer of wealth in the nation's history. More than 50% of that money will be in highly appreciated stocks, real estate or other property subject to capital gains taxation. With retirement and estate planning becoming high priorities for both wealthy and middle-income Americans, they will be forced to develop new and innovative ideas if they are to recapture some of those tax dollars.

At the same time, the number of qualified charitable organizations is increasing each year (accounting for ⅓ of our gross national product). Decreases in federal funding, increasing operating expenses, and a gradual decline in dollars gifted by wealthy estates (from 12.3% in 1976 to 6.3% in 1990) have fueled competition for charitable donations and forced nonprofits to search for alternatives.

More than 20 million Americans are already demonstrating charitable intent, and millions more are looking for ways to free up "frozen" assets by avoiding capital gains taxes on highly appreciated property. Charitable Remainder Trusts create that opportunity while coming to the aid of the nonprofit sector.

In the past, many have shied away from making a planned charitable gift due to concerns that they might need income from such an asset. CRTs allow them to retain income from that asset and draw a significant tax deduction from it, as well as receive the recognition and fulfillment of making such a gift in their lifetime. In other words, the donor decides the allocation of his income while continuing to draw from it through his retirement years. Everybody wins.

This easy-to-read, ground-breaking book guides you through the CRT process and outlines a marketing strategy from the perspective of an experienced planned giving specialist. In the pages ahead you will learn about:

- Different types of CRTs
- Popular uses of the CRT
- Prospects of the CRT
- Marketing the CRT
- How to set up a CRT
- Individual and business planning situations
- And more...

You will also discover the many ways CRTs benefit everyone from the casual investor and the financial professional to the nonprofit executive and those planning for retirement. You will learn of enlightening opportunities for those holding highly appreciated assets, building a strategy for a tax-free sale of a business or looking to expand their philanthropic resources.

Above all, this book is written to demonstrate that Charitable Remainder Trusts make sense, because they make money and make a difference for those committed to *do well by doing good.*

1

Laying the Foundation

There are many different reasons for making charitable contributions, and there are many different causes to contribute to. Some people donate out of compassion, others because they share a common interest. Whether it's education, the arts, science research or social service, most people give to make a difference, to contribute to the betterment of society.

The act of charitable giving in this country is complemented by a pattern of incentives that go beyond that of emotional fulfillment. Built around the tax system, these incentives reinforce the philosophy that it pays to give.

Deferred giving is perhaps the most common form of charitable giving. The word "deferred" is in some ways misleading, however, because it implies that the gift itself is deferred. Certainly, the charitable donee receives an immediate reward of interest in the donated property, but it is essentially only the donee's fulfillment of the gift that is deferred to a future time.

Planned Giving

- Bequests
- Revocable Trusts
- Life Insurance
- Pooled Income Fund
- Gift Annuity
- Charitable Remainder Trusts

An example might help better explain this basic concept. Suppose a 50-year-old investor inherits $200,000 of securities and adds them to her investment portfolio. According to her financial needs, she must retain an income from those securities for the rest of her life. Through her Will, she could leave the securities to a charitable organization upon her death.

Instead of making a bequest, however, she could make a gift of the remainder interest in the new securities to the charitable organization and retain the income interest for life. This is a deferred gift.

The end result leaves the donor receiving all the income from her securities throughout her life. Upon her death, the charitable organization retains full interest in the securities. She has basically divided the property into two parts — a life estate and a remainder interest.

A charitable gift such as this, however, does not yield a tax deduction from the income or gift (nor an estate tax charitable deduction if the gift is made at death). The Charitable Remainder Trust was established with the intent that such deferred gifts could draw tax benefits.

This philosophy of helping others while helping yourself is one that does not always reach those who are most

What is a Charitable Remainder Trust?

- An irrevocable tax-exempt trust
- Allows sale of highly appreciated assets without capital gains taxation
- Provides source of lifetime income
- Benefits investor's favorite nonprofit organizations

likely to reap its rewards. It is estimated that seven out of 10 Americans die without leaving a Will. Deferred gifts like the example mentioned above are often part of a larger plan, but many potential donors are under the mistaken impression that such planning is only for the affluent.

In fact, it could be said that planning for retirement and/or for the well-being of heirs once you've passed on is even more critical for middle-income Americans who cannot afford to absorb any mistakes in planning. On top of that, much of the value in a charitable gift that begins with a Will is diminished through government taxes and administrative fees.

Planned Giving Arrangements are just that, planned lifetime or ongoing gifts to charitable organizations and institutions within the structure of a long-term strategic plan. Not only do Planned Giving Arrangements match donors with a charity that meets the benefits of a tax deduction, but it forges a relationship that meets the specific needs of both charity and donor.

Planned Giving Arrangements can include ongoing cash or outright gifts, bargain sales, gift annuities, lead trusts, remainder interest in personal residents, Wills, gifts through life insurance and others.

Potential Tax Benefits of a CRT

- Income tax deduction
- Capital gains tax avoided
- Estate tax savings
- Tax-deferred growth

Many people make these types of ongoing gifts to organizations such as their local church, YMCA, alumni clubs and children's programs.

The Charitable Remainder Trust is one aspect of Planned Giving Arrangements. But, again, what separates a CRT from other forms of ongoing planned gifts is that it enables the donors to leverage their gifts.

If you have a good portion of your assets in your home, real estate and/or appreciated securities, a CRT can act as a vehicle that allows you to continue to support your favorite nonprofit charity while providing you income for the rest of your lifetime.

A CRT allows you, rather than the government, to control your social capital. If we define the money we earn, spend and live on as Personal Financial Capital, then Social Capital is what we pay in the form of taxes. Through taxes, the government decides where to spend your Social Capital. But with a CRT, you decide where your taxable income goes, whether toward social welfare programs, community organizations or other worthy charities.

Specifically, a CRT is a trust arrangement under which the trust creator, or donor, places an asset (usually highly appreciated) into an irrevocable trust for investment by a trustee.

In most situations, the income generated from the trust must be paid at least annually (exceptions to this rule will be discussed later) to the named beneficiaries, which usually includes the donor and spouse.

This annual payment continues through their lifetime, or a desired time period of no more than 20 years. Upon the death of the last income beneficiary or expiration of the time period selected, the remainder interest in the trust is paid to a non-taxable charity selected by the donor.

Although CRTs have been around since 1969, they've gained in popularity due to changes in the country's economic resources and recent media coverage illustrating its successes.

The January 14, 1996, issue of *The New York Times*, for example, featured an article on The Jackie Onassis Trust, in which the late First Lady had established a combination of a Charitable Lead Trust and a Charitable Remainder Trust. The article pointed out that "such an arrangement can be especially useful for older people holding stocks that have appreciated greatly but pay only a small dividend."

Because the after-tax proceeds of these shares might not yield a healthy return, many people might be hesitant to sell their shares. But with a Charitable Remainder Trust, the public or private charity of your choice can avoid capital gains taxation, sell your appreciated assets and reinvest the proceeds. This adds up to a larger income stream for the donor.

Charitable Remainder Trusts have been typically marketed as an estate planning tool along with advanced gifting techniques and planned giving. Even those in the business of marketing similar techniques have considered the Charitable Remainder Trust a sophisticated vehicle handled only by specialists and reserved for donors with unique circumstances.

1969 Tax Reform Act

- Charitable trusts became tax-exempt
- Current tax deduction for Present Value of future remainder interest
- Nonprofits and charities defined

While the CRT is indeed sophisticated, often requiring specific trust design and administrative services, it is a technique whose advantages and benefits can no longer be ignored — by trust professionals, planned giving specialists or donors.

This recent gain in exposure has helped to reveal the simplicity that is often hidden by the CRT's sophisticated reputation. Marketing, establishing and administering a CRT require a team approach that includes the potential donor. Let's continue to examine how CRTs help the whole team win.

2

Why Haven't I Heard About CRTs?

Perhaps the number one reason most people have never heard of the Charitable Remainder Trust is because very few planned giving specialists and financial advisors have been trained to maneuver around the complexities of the CRT to market its plain and simple advantages.

Another reason, of course, is the reluctance on the part of donors to consider investing in a charity while planning for their own future. This perception is often fueled by the giving specialist or financial advisor who hesitates in outlining the advantages of making planned gifts today.

The truth is, if marketed and presented properly, the Charitable Remainder Trust is a giving technique that is proving quite attractive to more and more donors. Once they learn that their charitable contributions can do as much for their own financial gain as that of their selected charity, they are interested in learning more. When they learn that their planned gifts can not only provide for their own retirement but, in some cases, provide income for

Why Haven't I Heard About CRTs Until Now?

- Multiple parties involved
  — Financial consultant
  — Attorney
  — Accountant
  — Trustee
  — Gift administrator
  — and you!
- Specialized trust administration
- Complex tax accounting

their heirs, they wonder, "Why haven't I heard of this before?"

In fact, in some cases it is the donors themselves who broach the subject of this unique aspect of planned giving.

I was conducting an estate and charitable planning seminar at a very affluent senior living facility. Before me was an audience of seniors who I knew could benefit from such a discussion.

I began to discuss the process to proper estate planning and how to insure the ease of passing one's assets with the least amount of cost and time delay.

That didn't seem to interest any of them nearly as much as the idea of planned giving. Many of the residents said that they had already done some estate planning, but told me the idea of charitable planning had never been suggested by financial advisors.

As I continued my discussion about how certain charitable giving techniques could be used, it was the Charitable

Remainder Trust that was most well-received. Most of my audience had never heard of the CRT.

It became apparent that the eye-opener to them was that the CRT provided them a way to give today, while they were alive to see the impact of their gift.

Of course, there were concerns about whether this type of giving threatened their current financial health. But in demonstrating the process of the CRT, I was able to show them that their financial status was not only protected by a CRT, but it could be enhanced by such a plan.

Many of the seniors went on to tell me they were currently giving to their church, a local charity, an alumni association or other organization. But they also told me they wanted to give more. Others said they planned on leaving money or gifts through their Wills.

I continued to share with them the concept of planned giving through the Charitable Remainder Trust. I was able to illustrate the way it worked through real life situations, and how they could receive all the living benefits they desired for the promise of a future gift.

In other words, by announcing and setting up their giving plans now, they would be afforded benefits from the promise of that future gift.

Of all the benefits I laid out concerning the Charitable Remainder Trust, these seniors seemed most excited about the fact that the CRT provided them the opportunity to give while they were still alive to experience the rewards of satisfaction, gratification and recognition that come with good philanthropy.

3

How a CRT Works

While the benefits of utilizing a Charitable Remainder Trust far outweigh the complexities of the process, the key to marketing this powerful giving tool involves a delicate balance of the two.

In the chapters ahead, we will continue to explore productive marketing strategies of the Charitable Remainder Trust to a variety of prospects. But first, you have to know how it works.

The chart on page 12 outlines the typical flow of assets in a Charitable Remainder Trust. The distribution of wealth primarily involves a five-step process:

1. Typically, the donor transfers highly appreciated asset(s) to the trust that has a low-cost basis and is producing minimal income. The most common assets are publicly traded stock and debt-free real estate.
2. After the assets are transferred to the trust, they can then be sold. The proceeds of a sale are exempt from

How Does a Charitable Remainder Trust Work?

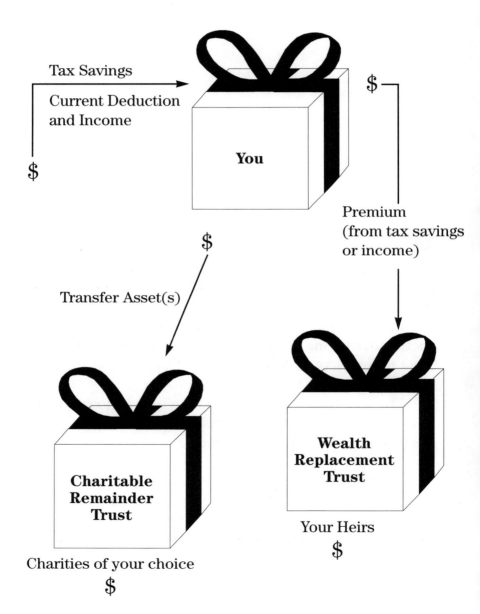

Tax Savings

Current Deduction and Income

$

You

$

Premium (from tax savings or income)

Transfer Asset(s)

$

Charitable Remainder Trust

Charities of your choice

$

Wealth Replacement Trust

Your Heirs

$

capital gains tax because the trust itself is not subject to income tax.

3. The proceeds are reinvested in a vehicle which generates an increased income for the income beneficiaries. The income can be paid for the duration of one or more lives, a term of years (not to exceed 20), or a combination of lives and years. The most common payment period is the lifetime of the donor and spouse, but strict regulations must be followed in setting up any time period.

4. Transferring the assets to the CRT generates a current tax deduction. An IRS formula is used to determine the "future value of a present gift." The formula takes into account the present value of the gift, the donor's age and the payout percentage selected. These criteria determine the value of the gift that will actually be received by the designated charity at some time in the future. The donor can deduct up to 50% of current adjusted gross income for cash contributions and 30% for appreciated gifts. The donor can carry forward any unused portion of the tax deduction for five years.

5. A CRT used in conjunction with an irrevocable life insurance trust, known as a Wealth Replacement Trust, permits the donor to make a gift to a charity in addition to providing for his or her heirs. The premium can often be paid from the tax savings generated by the charitable tax deduction and/or portion of the income from the trust.

There are three good reasons for setting up a Wealth Replacement Trust with a Charitable Remainder Trust:

1. Competition has forced insurers to offer contracts with better returns;

Wealth Replacement

- A side trust that replaces the asset values that go to the charities so your children and heirs are provided for
- Present value of future re-mainder interest creates current tax deduction
- Tax deduction sufficient in most cases to fund a life policy in a side trust

2. Earnings inside the contract are building tax-free; and
3. Proceeds are exempt from estate taxes.

A CRT with a net-income and make-up provision funded with the appropriate investment enables those who don't need current income to defer it for a period of time, until they elect to take income out. But many times, the instinct of an investor is to avoid a financial strategy that includes charitable giving because it usually means there is some disinheritance involved.

A Wealth Replacement Trust employed in an irrevocable life insurance trust eliminates those concerns in replacing those assets to the family on a tax-free basis.

From an estate planning standpoint, those assets have been taken from the estate, in effect reducing the estate tax liability. This enables the investor to pass on to heirs 100% of

Charitable Tax Deduction

The deduction is based on:
— Term of trust
— Contribution amount
— Payout rate
— Federal midterm rate

what they gave away, and either take a portion of the premium coming from the trust in buying that second life insurance contract or the irrevocable life insurance trust.

At the same time, the investor is offering tremendous support to a charitable organization today.

Small business owners may be the most likely candidates to capitalize on the recent emergence of the CRT. Statistics show that 70% to 80% of a business owner's income will come from the sale of that business. When it comes time to sell such a business, CRTs, in effect, guarantee to increase the value of that business. They also provide the business owner with a vehicle in which to sell their business tax-free, which means they collect more in annual income.

Many physicians possessing excessive funds find themselves in a similar situation. They may be capped in their 401K or IRA pension plans that limit how much they can put away. Through the CRT, they can put away as much as they like and get a tax deduction every time they fund their own retirement account or wealth accumulation fund.

Different types of CRTs fit different financial situations. These specialized options and their ability to save for the future demonstrate why Charitable Remainder Trusts are expected to be the wave of the future.

4

Different Types of CRTs

There are three types of CRTs: a "unitrust," called a Charitable Remainder Unitrust (CRUT); a "fixed annuity" trust, called a Charitable Remainder Annuity Trust (CRAT); and a "Pooled Income Fund."

The **CRUT** pays a fixed percentage (at least 5%) of the value of the asset(s) held in the trust based upon the *annual valuation*. Additional contributions are permitted and the income pay-out fluctuates in direct proportion to the annual trust value.

More simply, the requirements of a unitrust are:

- The unitrust must pay a fixed percentage, not less than 5%, of the net fair market value of its assets to one or more beneficiaries, at least one of which is not a charitable organization; in the case of an individual beneficiary, the individual must be living at the time the unitrust is created.

17

Types of
Charitable Remainder Trusts

Annuity = Fixed income
vs.
Unitrust = Variable income

- Standard
- Net income
- Net income with make-up

- The payment of the fixed percentage amount must be made either for a term of years (but not more than 20 years), or, in the case of an individual beneficiary(ies), for the life or lives of those individuals.
- The unitrust may pay no other amount to or for the use of any person other than a qualified charitable organization.
- When payments of the fixed percentage amounts terminate, the remainder of the unitrust either must be transferred to or for the use of a qualified charitable organization or must be retained by the unitrust for such use.

There are three types of CRUTs:

1. *Standard*, which pays out the fixed percentage of the annual trust value, regardless of the amount of trust earnings.
2. *Net Income*, which pays out the fixed percentage of the annual trust value or annual income, whichever is less.

CHARITABLE REMAINDER UNITRUST
Comparison Report
Gift vs. No Gift

Donor's Name: John Donor

Gift Information

Value of Gift	$1,000,000.00
Date of Gift	2/7/96
Type of Gift Asset	Stock
Cost Basis	$250,000.00
Fixed Unitrust Percentage	6.0000%
Payment Frequency	Quarterly
Full Months until First Payment	3
Length of Trust	Lifetimes of Beneficiaries
Beneficiaries' Ages	60, 50
Federal Interest Rate Used	6.8% (February 1996)
Charitable Deduction	$185,670.00

Gift Comparison

The following information is useful if the donor wishes to examine the potential income difference between making a gift to a Charitable Remainder Unitrust and keeping the asset:

	Gift	*No Gift*
1. Value of Gift	$1,000,000.00	$1,000,000.00
2. Charitable Deduction	$185,670.00	$0.00
3. Value of Deduction	$73,525.32	$0.00
(39.6% Tax Bracket)		
4. Donor's Investment	$926,474.68	$1,000,000.00
(Line 1 – Line 3)		
5. Income (%)	6.0000%	3.0000%
6. Income ($)	$60,000.00	$30,000.00
7. Effective Yield	6.4762%	3.0000%
(Line 6 ÷ Line 4)		
8. Increased Yield with Gift	115.8733%	

No planned gift should be made in the absence of a charitable intent or solely on the basis of financial expectations.

3. *Net-Income-with-Make-Up (NIMCRUT)*, which pays out the fixed percentage of the annual trust value or annual income, whichever is less, and permits use of past income deficiencies in subsequent years when the trust earns more than the required payout. Primarily due to its tremendous flexibility, the NIM-CRUT is the most popular of the Charitable Remainder Trusts. There are a number of benefits to funding a NIMCRUT with an annuity as compared to other common investments, which will be outlined in chapter six.

The fixed percentage payout of the CRUT must be paid at least annually, for the lifetime of the income beneficiary(ies) or for a fixed term of years.

The **CRAT** pays a fixed percentage (at least 5%) of the *initial value* of the assets on the date of transfer to the trust. While additional contributions to the trust are prohibited, the income remains constant regardless of the value of the trust assets or investment performance. It does not provide for inflation.

If the trust earnings are not sufficient to meet the income payout obligation, the trustee is forced to invade trust principal. With this in mind, the IRS has denied an estate tax charitable deduction when, by its calculations, there is more than a remote possibility (5%) that the trust would have no assets remaining to distribute to the charity.

Current income tax deductions might likewise be jeopardized in such a case. IRS software programs automatically run the "5% Probability Test."

To put it more simply, to qualify as a CRAT, a trust must meet the following requirements:

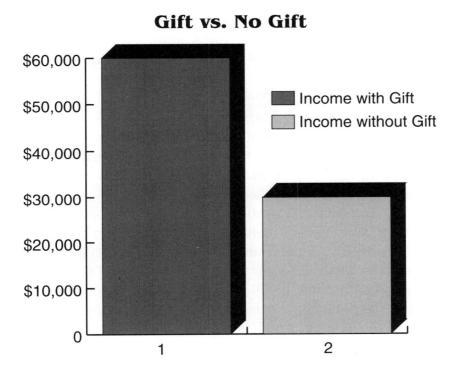

Gift vs. No Gift

- The trust must pay a sum certain to at least one non-charitable beneficiary; in the case of an individual beneficiary, the individual must be living at the time the trust is created.
- The sum certain that is paid cannot be less than 5% of the initial net fair market value of the property placed in the trust.
- The sum certain must be payable, at least annually, either for a term of years (no more than 20) or for the life or lives of the noncharitable beneficiary(ies).
- The trust may pay no other amounts to or for the use of any person other than a qualified charitable organization.

- When payment of the sum certain terminates, the remainder interest either must be transferred to or for the use of a qualified charitable organization or must be retained by the trust for such use.

How the specified distributions to the beneficiaries are determined is essentially what distinguishes whether a CRT is a Charitable Remainder Unitrust (CRUT) or a Charitable Remainder Annuity Trust (CRAT). The value of an investment inside of a CRUT or CRAT may vary depending upon the gift or asset. The financial profile on the opposite page reveals how they both might compare to a stock value of $1 million.

A **Pooled Income Trust** allows irrevocable gifts from separate donors to be commingled for investment purposes. Each named income beneficiary receives a proportionate share of the net income earned by the fund each year. At the death of the income beneficiary, the portion of the fund representing the value of the units assigned to that income beneficiary is distributed to the charity.

Pooled income funds are somewhat similar to mutual funds. These funds pool the contributions of several donors into one large trust. This trust is managed by the charitable organization and each of the donors is paid from the trust's earnings on a share basis. Contributions to a pooled income fund are deductible for income tax purposes and offer guaranteed income for the life of the donor. Not all charitable organizations are eligible for pooled income donations, and the donor cannot be the trustee.

There are significant differences between pooled income funds and CRUTs and CRATs. The requirements of a pooled income fund include:

- The donor must transfer an irrevocable remainder interest in property to or for the use of certain organi-

Husband and Wife, Age 60 and 50
Comparison Sale of Stock and
Transfer to CRT

	Stock	CRAT	CRUT
Stock Value	$1,000,000	$1,000,000	$1,000,000
Capital Gain on Sale	$750,000	0	0
Tax on Gain (28%)	$210,000	0	0
Amount Invested	$790,000	$1,000,000	$1,000,000
Charitable Deduction	0	$237,940	$185,670
Assumed Tax Benefit			
@ 39.6% (1)	0	$94,225	$73,525
Total Funds Invested	$790,000	$1,094,225	$1,073,525
Annual Income @ 6%	$47,400	$65,655	$64,410 (2)
Incremental Over Sale	N/A	$18,255	$17,010
		39%	36%
Balance of Estate	$790,000	$94,225	$73,525
Federal Estate Tax			
@ 55%	$434,500	$51,825	$40,440
Net to Family	$355,500	$42,400	$33,085
Net Cost to Family	N/A	$313,100	$322,415
Value to Charity	0	$1,000,000	$1,000,000
Total to Family			
and Charity	$355,500	$1,042,400	$1,033,085

Assumes Feb '96 AFR: 6.8%
(1) Held outside the trust
(2) Will increase with growth of value of trust

zations, contributions to which qualify for the 50% income tax charitable deduction, and must retain an income interest in the property for the life or lives of one or more beneficiaries.

- The property transferred must be commingled with property transferred by other donors.
- The fund can neither receive as a contribution, nor invest in tax-exempt securities.
- The fund can include only those amounts received from transfers that meet the requirements for pooled income funds.
- The fund must be maintained by the organization to which the remainder interest is contributed and cannot have a donor or a beneficiary of an income interest as a trustee.
- The income received each year by the income beneficiary must be determined by the rate of return earned by the fund for such year.

While the pooled income trust may be the most effective vehicle in certain situations, this book focuses primarily on the use of a unitrust and an annuity within a CRT.

5

Popular Uses of CRTs

While there are a number of uses and benefits in creating a specific type of Charitable Remainder Trust, the most common CRT strategy is planned through the Charitable Remainder Unitrust (CRUT).

Again, we defined the CRUT as one that pays a fixed percentage of the value of the asset(s) held in the trust based upon an *annual valuation*. And as we said, the three types of CRUTs include Standard, Net Income, and Net-Income-with-Make-Up (NIMCRUT).

Because most CRUT prospects are looking to convert valuable assets into economic gain, retirement money and/or education funds for children or grandchildren, it's no surprise that the four most popular uses, or "vehicles," of a CRUT are: the *asset conversion vehicle*, the *retirement vehicle*, the *education vehicle* and the *estate vehicle*.

These strategic avenues enable donors to realize their financial goals and, as illustrated in the examples that follow, often result in benefits they may not have originally imagined.

Asset Conversion Vehicle: Increasing Income While Avoiding Capital Gains Tax

Asset conversion is the most popular use of a CRUT. The client owns a highly appreciated debt-free asset which has a low-cost basis and is producing minimal income. Once an asset is transferred to a CRUT, it can be sold and the proceeds will avoid capital gains tax. The full amount of the proceeds can then be reinvested in an asset producing a higher income.

One example of utilizing an asset conversion vehicle involves an 82-year-old man who approached me at an estate and charitable planning seminar I conducted in Florida. The audience was made up of very affluent residents of the same senior living facility I mentioned earlier, where the rates ranged from $3,500 to $5,000 a month.

The gentleman began to tell me that he owned some land in New Jersey, which he purchased in 1974. Because he wasn't sure if he'd ever make it back to Jersey, he said he'd like to sell his land and give it to his local church in Florida.

The man wanted to know if he could do that through a Charitable Remainder Trust. Before answering, I asked him to tell me a little more about this land. Was it raw land? Was it rental property? He said he wasn't sure exactly what he had, but he received a check every month ranging from between $7,000 and $9,000. He said he actually only needed about $1,500 of that amount each month.

Now, anything that's producing $84,000 to $108,000 has got to be one heck of a piece of land. When I asked him who sends him the check, he told me it was a management company. He said his brother-in-law was involved with the property and hired this management company to handle administrative duties.

Before going any further, I suggested we call this company to find out what we're talking about here. We found out that the land this fellow bought in 1974 for $38,000 sits on the inter-coastal waterway on the south shore of the state. It housed a marina with 119 boat slips valued at approximately $4.2 million. This news made the gentleman even that much more excited about giving the property to his church.

Of course, I asked, "What about that brother-in-law of yours?" The gentleman said, "The heck with him, he's probably what led my sister to an early grave."

The man wound up selling the marina inside the Asset Conversion Vehicle of the CRT, received a healthy tax deduction, bypassed any capital gains tax, received a lifetime income and became a hero of sorts among the members of that little Florida church. Who knows what happened to the brother-in-law.

Retirement Vehicle:
Building A Retirement Fund

A CRUT is an ideal vehicle for professionals and business owners building a retirement fund or seeking a supplement to their qualified plan. Under qualified plans (defined benefit, defined contribution, 401K, IRAs, etc.), annual contributions are limited. With a CRUT, there are no annual contribution limits. A client receives an annual charitable tax deduction for each year they make a contribution.

Many business owners hesitate to sell their business because of concerns over tax implications. Here are some examples of how CRT retirement vehicles help alleviate those concerns.

The greatest potential for growth in CRTs may be through the application of a supplemental pension plan. Think for a moment about the purpose of an IRA, 401K, defined benefit plan, 403B and all the other retirement plans. What is their purpose? To provide the participant income through retirement years. Right?

Well, the Charitable Remainder Trust can do that, without the restrictions and rules governing qualified plans.

Let's look at some real life practical applications and the markets most suitable for this tax-deductible, non-qualified private pension plan.

Small businesses or business owners

Most financial professionals, whether they are marketing a product or services to this group, are pretty much offering the same thing — IRAs, 401K, Keoghs and maybe group employee benefits. Most small businesses are experiencing a lot of the same higher operating expenses, diminishing profit margins, and increasing employee turnover.

So the idea of incurring additional expenses to fund an employee benefit may not seem too appealing in a business environment where uncertainty looms over whether an employee will show up at work tomorrow — let alone still be there 10 or 20 years from tomorrow.

What if there were a way to provide the small business owner a tax-deductible, non-qualified, private pension plan that allows him to discriminate against the funding of other retirement accounts to the uncertain employee, with no limits on how much to put away and secure for his comfortable retirement? Let me repeat: a non-qualified, tax-deductible, private pension plan with no limits that lets the small business owner determine who can participate — would you be interested? By the way, this strategy would also increase the value of the business.

What is the only intangible asset that appears on a balance sheet? Goodwill. How you value goodwill is uncertain at best. But if you, the small business owner, could document every time you funded your private pension plan, earmarking your retirement dollars to go to your local church, hospital, alumni association, YMCA or other charity, not only would you have received the tax deduction every time you funded it, but it helps increase the value of the business. That's what a Charitable Remainder Trust can do if it's used as a retirement vehicle.

Considering that 70% to 80% of a business owner's income at retirement will come from the sale of that business, the CRT becomes an invaluable tool in securing a comfortable retirement.

Sale of a business

Another area in which the CRT has become a great ally is in the sale of a business. In this day and age of growing competition and consolidation, an owner has to anticipate an exit-out strategy to maximize the value of his business at the time of sale.

With many managed care companies actively buying up small medical practices, physicians with their own practices are feeling the pressures of change as much as anyone. They too are facing higher operating costs, diminishing profit margins, and increasing liability premiums. They are being tantalized by these large managed care facilities and hospitals who approach like white knights willing to save them from the perils of individual practices.

A large number of doctors are finding the idea of somebody else covering their costs and absorbing some of their liability quite appealing. Along with the promise of a steady cash flow, doctors are selling these small businesses in record numbers. But if we take a closer look, there may be a better option.

Let's say Dr. Fracture has operated his medical practice for 30 years and is now being solicited for purchase by a managed health care facility. The company offers $1 million for his practice. If sold outright, he would be facing a tax liability on $1 million; some of it would be taxed as capital gains depending on the capital invested and cost basis, the rest as ordinary income.

Let's hypothetically suggest the doctor pays 30% in taxes, leaving him with $700,000 after-tax to be re-invested at 6%. That would generate a $42,000 yearly income while incurring a $300,000 tax liability. Dr. Fracture is not likely to be interested in that option because he spends that much in pocket change.

The managed care facility then counters with an offer of $100,000 a year with a special interest arrangement for the next 10 years. Well, Dr. Fracture thinks this isn't so bad. Now, he has increased his income, but it is taxed as ordinary income on $100,000. The question then becomes, is this the best time value of money, and how secure are the future payments if something were to happen to the managed health care company?

A better idea might be to establish a CRT, transfer the business into the trust and sell the business in the tax-exempt trust for $1 million. With this option, not only will Dr. Fracture avoid paying the approximately $300,000 in taxes, he will get a significant tax deduction to offset his current income tax liability. Now he has $1 million to reinvest at 6%, which is now $60,000 and may actually be tax-free based on the tax deduction. He maintains an asset base of $1 million to receive a lifetime income stream or, in some cases, he can let it grow until needed.

This is where hospital foundations and development offices could really do well by doing good and provide a substantial employee benefit.

CHARITABLE REMAINDER UNITRUST
Comparison Report
Gift vs. Sell and Reinvest

Donor's Name: John Donor

Gift Information

Value of Gift	$1,000,000.00
Date of Gift	2/7/96
Type of Gift Asset	Stock
Cost Basis	$250,000.00
Fixed Unitrust Percentage	6.0000%
Payment Frequency	Quarterly
Full Months until First Payment	3
Length of Trust	Lifetimes of Beneficiaries
Beneficiaries' Ages	60, 50
Federal Interest Rate Used	6.8% (February 1996)
Charitable Deduction	$185,670.00

Gift Comparison

The following information is useful if the donor wishes to examine the potential income difference between making a gift to a Charitable Remainder Unitrust and selling the asset and reinvesting the income:

		Gift	*Sell & Reinvest*
1.	Value of Gift	$1,000,000.00	$1,000,000.00
2.	Charitable Deduction	$185,670.00	$0.00
3.	Value of Deduction (39.6% Tax Bracket)	$73,525.32	$0.00
4.	Donor's Investment	$926,474.68	$1,000,000.00
5.	Capital Gain	$750,000.00	$750,000.00
6.	Capital Gains Tax Paid (28% Tax Bracket)	$0.00	$210,000.00
7.	Investment Amount (Line 1 – Line 6)	$1,000,000.00	$790,000.00
8.	Reinvested Income (%)	6.0000%	6.0000%
9.	Reinvested Income ($)	$60,000.00	$47,400.00
10.	Effective Yield (Line 9 ÷ Line 4)	6.4762%	4.7400%
11.	Increased Yield with Gift	36.6287%	

No planned gift should be made in the absence of a charitable intent or solely on the basis of financial expectations.

Here's another quick example of a retirement vehicle. Let's say Mr. Fixit started a business in his garage in 1952 with a $5,000 loan from his life insurance policy. Today, the business is worth $1,500,000 and he owns more than 50% of the stock.

If he sells the interest to an outsider, or the corporation (and other stockholders agree to retire their stock), Mr. Fixit is looking at a reportable capital gain of well over $1,000,000. That's a tough way to enter retirement bliss.

But, Mr. Fixit might have a better option. If he puts his stock into a CRT retirement vehicle, he can reserve an income for life. The trust could sell the stock, if there is no binding agreement requiring the trustee to sell, and avoid reporting the immediate capital gain. Now, the trustee of the CRT can diversify this capital into high yielding, secure investments suitable for retirement cash flow.

Whether building toward retirement for the business owner or maximizing at retirement, the CRT can become a powerful planning technique for wealth accumulation and wealth preservation toward securing a comfortable retirement.

Education Vehicle: Building A College Fund

A CRUT is also an ideal way to build a college fund for children and/or grandchildren. The donor is entitled to a charitable tax deduction when the trust is established. Income is usually deferred until the student(s) start college and is then paid out over the years they are enrolled. Additionally, the income is taxed at the student's tax bracket rather than the higher tax bracket of the donor.

CHARITABLE REMAINDER UNITRUST
Cash Flow Projection

Donor's Name: John Donor

Gift Information

Value of Gift	$250,000.00
Date of Gift	2/8/96
Type of Gift Asset	Property
Cost Basis	$50,000.00
Fixed Unitrust Percentage	10.0000%
Payment Frequency	Quarterly
Full Months until First Payment	3
Length of Trust	Term of 4 Years
Beneficiary's Age	18
Federal Interest Rate Used	6.8% (February 1996)
Charitable Deduction	$166,970.00

Growth Assumptions

Donor's Tax Bracket	39.6%
Beneficiary's Tax Bracket	15.0%
Expected Total Return	8.0000%
Number of Years Shown	4
Income Shown	Before Tax

Cash Flow Projection

End of Year	Principal	Income
1	245,000.00	25,000.00
2	240,100.00	24,500.00
3	235,298.00	24,010.00
4	230,592.04	23,529.80
Total:	230,592.04	97,039.80

Using a CRT as leverage for college planning can come in a variety of ways. I recall being asked to make a CRT presentation before a man who was perceived to be an ideal candidate. The man held approximately $484,000 worth of stock in an insurance company. His cost basis was $17,000 and he wanted to sell the stock and diversify his holdings, but he didn't want to pay the capital gains taxes due upon the sale.

When I visited the man at his rather magnificent home, I wondered if he had ever given any thought to charitable giving. As I began to expound on the virtues of charitable planned giving and probe him for where his charitable interest might lie, I quickly learned he did not have any charitable interests.

Just as I shifted my presentation toward the more economic reasoning behind CRTs, I saw a teenage girl enter the side door of the man's home. Remembering the old adage, "Charity begins at home," I latched onto an even more promising approach.

When I asked the man where he attended college, he proudly responded with the name of a prominent Ivy League institution. I said, "Great school. Do you support the alumni?" "No," he barked back, "they've done nothing for me." Then I asked him the loaded question, "Do you have any children?" He told me he had a daughter in high school, obviously the young woman I had just seen. When I asked if he hoped she would attend the same Ivy League school, he told me she'd be lucky to graduate from high school.

"If there were a way to improve your daughter's chances of getting into that university," I asked him, "while you received a tax deduction upon her acceptance and an income to pay for her education, would you be interested?" All of the sudden, the man became very interested and we began exploring how the Charitable Remainder Trust could afford him these opportunities.

With a CRT, not only would he be able to sell his stock and bypass capital gains taxes, he could get a tax deduction, reinvest the proceeds of the trust into a diversified portfolio and earmark these future funds to go to the university upon his death. Through this type of planning, he was convinced he could accomplish a number of important objectives. The hardest part might have been motivating his daughter to improve her academic standing so that the rest of the pieces could fall into place.

In approaching the university's foundation department and offering this strategy as a future gift, his daughter was accepted to the school and he was named to the board of the foundation.

In essence, the Charitable Remainder Trust not only allowed him to gain economic benefit from bypassing the capital gains taxes, it enabled him to receive a sizable tax deduction and a lifetime income from the trust. It also helped secure his daughter's continued education and, in the process, it helped the man discover he was quite a philanthropist.

Estate Vehicle:
Making the Most of an ESOP

A CRT/ESOP (Employment Stock Ownership Plan) is a method by which a shareholder of a private, closely held company (donor) may gift company stock to a charity which would in turn sell the stock to the company's ESOP.

Using a Charitable Remainder Trust, the patron transfers assets to a trust and retains lifetime income from the trust. Upon the termination of the trust, the principal passes to the charitable organization(s) of the patron's choice. CRTs are very popular in this area due to the elimination of alternative tax strategies.

In effect, this type of transaction will allow the selling shareholder to receive a lifetime income, save shareholder gains, create a gift deduction and reduce taxable estate.

The CRT will name the husband or wife, or both, as the beneficiary of the trust's income (usually a percent of the market value) and one or more charities as the beneficiaries of the principal amount upon the death of the surviving spouse.

The Wealth Replacement Trust in this case allows the gifted asset to be preserved, estate tax free, for the donor's family or other beneficiaries. The trust would own a life insurance policy on the life of the donor (or spouse) so that the gifted asset remains in the estate free of estate taxes. The chart on page 37 demonstrates the flow of cash through the CRT/ESOP with a Wealth Replacement Trust.

The steps and effects of establishing a CRT/ESOP are rather simple, while the benefits are rather impressive. Below, we outline the process and projected outcome of this estate vehicle.

Steps of a CRT/ESOP:

1. Shareholder gifts company stock to Charitable Remainder Trust (CRT).
2. CRT sells stock to ESOP; ESOP acquires loan from lending institution.
3. Funds from stock sale to ESOP flow back to CRT.
4. Income to shareholder from investment by CRT; shareholder sets up Wealth Replacement Trust.
5. Shareholder uses tax deduction and tax savings to purchase insurance policy for family benefit.
6. Family members or other beneficiaries receive at least amount of CRT gift upon shareholder's demise.

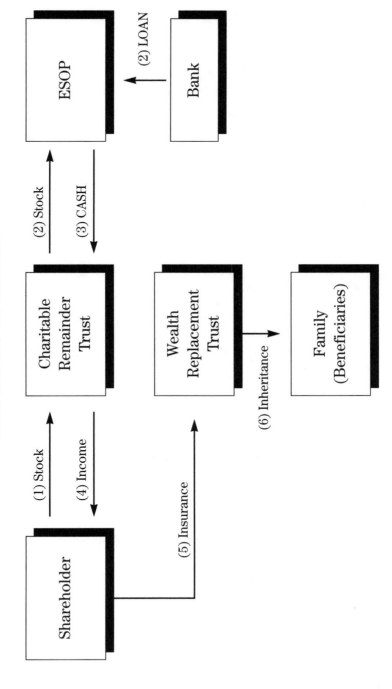

ESTATE PLANNING CHART
Movement of Income

ESOP

Bank

(2) LOAN

(2) Stock

(3) CASH

Charitable Remainder Trust

Wealth Replacement Trust

Family (Beneficiaries)

(6) Inheritance

(1) Stock

(4) Income

(5) Insurance

Shareholder

Effects of a CRT/ESOP:

1. No income tax by shareholder on gift to CRT.
2. ESOP receives funds through leverage loan, no limitation of ESOP allocations to shareholder or family.
3. No restriction on funds invested by CRT for income to shareholder.
4. Lifetime income to the shareholder; charity takes possession of gift with demise of shareholder.
5. Method to redeem gift amount from CRT for family benefit.
6. Family received inheritance from insurance policy upon demise of shareholder.

ESOP Benefits

The company will realize:

- Substantial tax savings
- Increased cash flow
- Increased net worth
- Use of pre-tax dollars to repay debt
- Tax deductible dividends
- Maximum employee motivation through participation

The stockholders will achieve:

- Liquidity for shares at fair market value
- Tax-free sale of stock
- Preservation of voting control
- Independent and continuing valuation of shares

Employees will enjoy:

- Meaningful retirement fund
- New sense of team spirit
- Opportunity to share in the growth of the company without a reduction in wages
- Continued operation and perpetuation of the company after the sale by principal owners

Let's take a look at an individual situation to better realize the difference a trust can make, and the importance of having a plan. On page 40 is a breakdown of Mr. Patron's financial situation.

In analyzing the numbers and their end result with and without a planned giving arrangement that includes a Charitable Remainder Trust, the significance of adopting a long-term strategy is made obvious.

Before delving into the use of a CRAT, let's look at a special use of a unitrust with benefits geared to provide for the donor's family.

Living Remainder Unitrust

The Living Remainder Unitrust is a qualified trust which pays income to family members. After all of the income payments have been completed, the remainder is distributed to qualified charities.

The person who establishes the trust may select the unitrust percentage, the persons to receive the income from the trust and the time for which the payments will be made, and the charities which will receive the principal of the trust after all income payments are completed.

$10,000,000
CHARITABLE TRUST ANALYSIS
Mr. Patron, age 60
Charitable Trust vs. No Charitable Trust

	No Planning	**Trust**
Living Benefits		
Asset Value	$10,000,000	$10,000,000
Capital Gains Tax (28%)	($2,800,000)	0
Net Value to Mr. Patron/Trust	$7,200,000	$10,000,000
Asset Available for Income	$7,200,000	$10,000,000
Income (10%)	$720,000	$1,000,000
Income Tax Deductible (25.5%)	0	$2,550,000
Death Benefits		
Estate Value	$7,200,000	$10,000,000
Estate Tax (55%)	($3,960,000)	0
Probate Expenses (3%)	($216,000)	0
To Patron's Heirs	$3,024,000	$10,000,000
Legacy Benefits		
Patron's Estate Value	$3,024,000	$10,000,000
Estate Tax (55%)	($1,663,200)	0
Probate Expenses (3%)	($90,720)	0
To Mr. & Mrs. Patron's Heirs	$1,270,080	$10,000,000

Unitrust Percentage

Each grantor may select the unitrust percentage. The unitrust percentage may amount to 5% more of the value of the trust. Each year the trust accountant determines the fair market value of the trust. The unitrust then pays the selected percent of the fair market value to the family.

For instance, if a trust is valued at $100,000 and the trust grantor selected a 6% unitrust percentage, the accountant would multiply the 6% by the $100,000 in value and distribute $6,000 that year. If earnings were 9% or 10% and the trust distributed 6%, the extra 3% or 4% would be added to the principal. Since the income payments depend upon the value in trust, many persons select a lower percentage and then benefit from the growth of the trust value during later years of the trust.

Duration of Income

In addition, the trust grantor may also select the time for which payments are able to be made. This time may be two lives, one life or a term of one to 20 years. The example on page 43 shows a trust which pays income for two lives. After both of the trust recipients have passed away, the trust **corpus** (principal) will then be distributed to charity.

Charitable Remainder

Finally, the trust grantor may select the charities that will receive the **trust remainder** (the corpus of the trust after all income payments are completed). The entire corpus could be distributed to one charity, or the corpus may be divided among several charities. The selection of the charities is entirely under the control of the trust grantor.

The major benefits of the trust are (i) bypass of capital gains tax, (ii) increased income and (iii) a charitable income tax deduction.

Bypass Capital Gains Tax

Investments of property eventually mature. After a very good investment has appreciated, the yield or earnings on that investment may then be quite low. At certain times, it is wise to sell a property and reinvest the proceeds in a new property for maximum investment gain.

The unitrust is an ideal method for a tax-free reinvestment, since the qualified unitrust bypasses the capital gains tax. The full amount received from the sale will then be reinvested.

Increased Income

Mature investment properties frequently are earning 2%, 3% or 4% per year. The capital gains tax-free reinvestment through the unitrust could enable a person to sell without tax an asset earning 2% or 3% and reinvest in an asset earning 9% or 10%. The increased earnings can then be passed through to the family members using the unitrust income produced by higher yield investments. Over a period of years, the family members can reinvest the additional income and acquire even greater economic security.

Income Tax Deduction

After the completion of all income payments, the corpus is distributed to charity. Even though the charity might not receive anything for many years, the government permits the trust grantor (the person who establishes the irrevocable trust) to take an immediate income tax deduction. The deduction is a percentage of the value of the property transferred to the trust and is calculated using the ages of the donors and the unitrust percentage selected. Many trust donors use their current tax savings for additional investments and thus are able to enjoy the maximum return from their tax-free reinvestment and also benefit at the same time from substantial income tax savings.

Trustee

Each unitrust must have a trustee. The trustee can be a commercial institution such as a bank or trust company, a charity, an individual or a combination of two of these three options. The trustee will have to invest the property, conduct any sales and file the appropriate information and tax forms. Since the trust may last for many years, it is important to select a trustee in whom the donor has confidence.

The following planning situation illustrates how a Living Remainder Unitrust can increase the income from an asset while causing a decrease in taxes.

Living Remainder Unitrust Situation:
Mr. & Mrs. Valued Client

Stock Portfolio — $500,000
Cost Basis — $50,000
Dividend (2%) — $10,000
Sold at — $450,000
Capital Gains Tax — $126,000
Net Available to Re-invest — $374,000

Mr. & Mrs. Valued Client desire more income and fewer taxes. What can we do?

The answer: Establish a Charitable Remainder Trust.

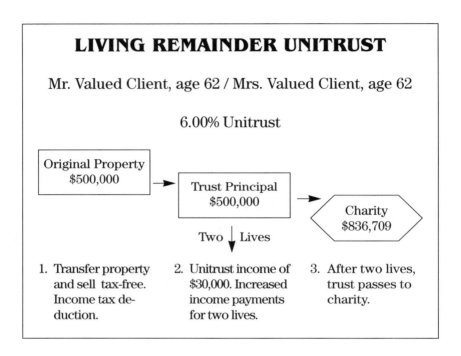

LIVING REMAINDER UNITRUST

Mr. Valued Client, age 62 / Mrs. Valued Client, age 62

6.00% Unitrust

Original Property
$500,000

Trust Principal
$500,000

Charity
$836,709

Two ↓ Lives

1. Transfer property and sell tax-free. Income tax deduction.

2. Unitrust income of $30,000. Increased income payments for two lives.

3. After two lives, trust passes to charity.

We defined the Charitable Remainder Annuity Trust (CRAT) as one which pays a fixed percentage of the initial value (as opposed to the annual valuation) of the assets on the date of the trust.

Often, those establishing a CRAT are average wage earners who are now up in years. They are not likely to have experienced an income tax problem or accumulated a large estate, but find satisfaction in small acts of generosity. Now, in the "sunset years" of their lives, with inflation nipping at their lifestyles, they plan the transfer of what wealth they have accumulated to their favorite charitable cause.

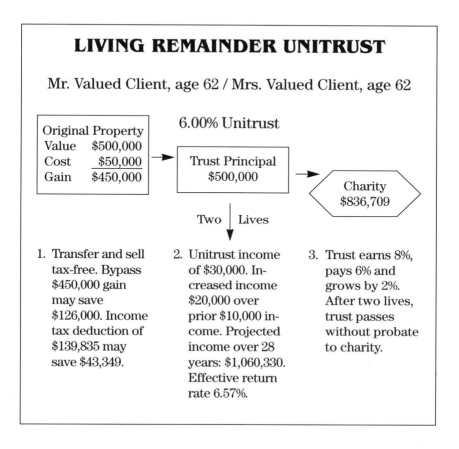

LIVING REMAINDER UNITRUST

Mr. Valued Client, age 62 / Mrs. Valued Client, age 62

6.00% Unitrust

Original Property
Value $500,000
Cost $50,000
Gain $450,000

Trust Principal
$500,000

Charity
$836,709

Two | Lives

1. Transfer and sell tax-free. Bypass $450,000 gain may save $126,000. Income tax deduction of $139,835 may save $43,349.

2. Unitrust income of $30,000. Increased income $20,000 over prior $10,000 income. Projected income over 28 years: $1,060,330. Effective return rate 6.57%.

3. Trust earns 8%, pays 6% and grows by 2%. After two lives, trust passes without probate to charity.

Looking for opportunities to maximize their charitable legacy, they discover new leverage in planned giving techniques. Perhaps they combine life estate and gift annuity techniques to transfer their personal residence to charity during their lifetimes, and they reserve the right to live there and receive additional income. Or, at age 80, they discover they can trade their bank certificate, yielding 3%, for a gift annuity guaranteeing 8.8%, and pass the principal to charity. Or, they find the opportunity to make an estate tax deductible testamentary transfer of their estate values or a percentage of it by Will or revocable trust.

TRUST BENEFITS FOR FAMILY AND CHARITY

YRS	PRINCIPAL 8.0% Ret. 2.0% Growth (1)	UT INCOME PAYMENTS 6.0% Pmt (2)	TOTAL OF UT INCOME PAYMENTS (3)	INCOME AFTER TAX 31.0% Tax (4)	INCOME TAX SAVINGS (5)	TOTAL OF BENEFITS AFTER TAX (6)
1	$500,000	$30,000	$30,000	$20,700	$43,349	$64,049
2	510,000	30,600	60,600	21,114	0	85,163
3	520,200	31,212	91,812	21,536	0	106,699
4	530,604	31,836	123,648	21,967	0	128,666
5	541,216	32,473	156,121	22,406	0	151,072
6	552,040	33,122	189,244	22,854	0	173,927
7	563,081	33,785	223,029	23,312		197,239
8	574,343	34,461	257,489	23,778		221,016
9	585,830	35,150	292,639	24,253		245,270
10	597,546	35,853	328,492	24,738		270,008
11	609,497	36,570	365,061	25,233		295,241
12	621,687	37,301	402,363	25,738		320,979
13	634,121	38,047	440,410	26,253		347,232
14	646,803	38,808	479,218	26,778		374,009
15	659,739	39,584	518,803	27,313		401,323
16	672,934	40,376	559,179	27,859		429,182
17	686,393	41,184	600,362	28,417		457,599
18	700,121	42,007	642,369	28,985		486,584
19	714,123	42,847	685,217	29,565		516,148
20	728,406	43,704	728,921	30,156		546,304
21	742,974	44,578	773,500	30,759		577,064
22	757,833	45,470	818,970	31,374		608,438
23	772,990	46,379	865,349	32,002		640,440
24	788,450	47,307	912,656	32,642		673,081
25	804,219	48,253	960,909	33,295		706,376
26	820,303	49,218	1,010,127	33,961		740,337
27	836,709	50,203	1,060,330	34,640		774,976
28	853,443	51,207	1,111,536	35,333		810,309
29	870,512	52,231	1,163,767	36,039		846,348
30	887,922	53,275	1,217,042	36,760		883,108
31	905,681	54,341	1,271,383	37,495		920,603
32	923,794	55,428	1,326,811	38,245		958,848
33	942,270	56,536	1,383,347	39,010		997,858
34	961,116	57,667	1,441,014	39,790		1,037,649
35	980,338	58,820	1,499,834	40,586		1,078,235
36	999,945	59,997	1,559,831	41,398		1,119,632
37	1,019,944	61,197	1,621,028	42,226		1,161,858
38	1,040,343	62,421	1,683,448	43,070		1,204,928
39	1,061,149	63,669	1,747,117	43,932		1,248,860
40	1,082,372	64,942	1,812,059	44,810		1,293,670

Expectancy:	27.8 years	Charitable Deduction:	$139,835
Total/Charity:	$836,709	Income Tax Savings:	$43,349
Benefits/Family:	$774,976	Allocated Basis:	$13,984
Type Income:	Ordinary	Alt. Min. Tax Pref.:	$125,852

CHARITABLE REMAINDER UNITRUST
Two Lives

Donor __Mr. Valued Client__ Gift Amount __$500,000__ Gift Date __02/01/93__

First Person __Mr. Valued Client__ Birth Date __01/01/31__ Age* __62__

Second Person __Mrs. Valued Client__ Birth Date __01/01/31__ Age* __62__

Payment Frequency __ANNUAL__ (Payments at end of selected period)

*Age — Year changes at six months from birth date.

(A)	Unitrust Percentage	6.00%	(A)
(B)	Factor for Adjusted Payout Rate IRS Pub. 1458, Table F AFR of the Month 7.6%	0.929368	(B)
(C)	Adjusted Payout Rate (A × B)	5.576%	(C)
(D)	Nearest table rate below (C)	5.40%	(D)
(E)	Factor at Line (D) rate [IRS Pub. 1458, Table U(2)]	0.29049	(E)
(F)	Nearest table rate above (C)	5.60%	(F)
(G)	Factor at Line (F) rate [IRS Pub. 1458, Table U(2)]	0.27819	(G)
(H)	Line (E) – Line (G)	0.01230	(H)
(I)	Line (C) – Line (D)	0.176%	(I)
(J)	Line (I) ÷ 0.2%	0.88000	(J)
(K)	Line (H) × Line (J)	0.01082	(K)
(L)	Line (E) – Line (K)	0.27967	(L)
(M)	Line (L) × Gift Amount PRESENT VALUE OF REMAINDER INTEREST	$139,835	(M)
(N)	TAX BRACKET AND SAVINGS 31.00%	$43,349	(N)

Let's say an 85-year-old donor holds a quantity of low yielding industrial stock. He plans to give his $600,000 Unified Credit equivalent to some grandnieces and nephews, and would rather give the balance to charity than to the government.

Rather than sell and pay capital gains tax, he asks about a charitable income plan. Because of his age, he is not looking at a long-term investment or payout. His best option to avoid being taxed would seem to be a gift annuity set up through a CRAT.

Perhaps the greatest benefit of CRTs is that "everybody wins!": the donor, the adviser, and the charity.

Donor Benefits:

- Increase current income
- Reduce current income taxes
- Eliminate capital gains tax on sale of appreciated asset
- Diversify assets
- Reduce estate taxes
- Satisfaction of benefiting charities
- Conserve estate for heirs and avoid probate (Wealth Replacement Trust)

Advisor Benefits:

- Unlock donor assets that are currently "untouchable"
- Enhance professional image
- Eliminate competition
- Move to more affluent clientele
- Generate continual stream of quality referrals
- Satisfaction of benefiting charities

Charity Benefits:

- Gifts through a CRT tend to be larger gifts
- Secure assets and donors that are not otherwise accessible
- Establish basis for additional future gifts

For an analysis of the advantages and disadvantages of the contribution techniques covered here, see the following page.

Comparison of Charitable Contribution Techniques

	Advantages	Disadvantages
Outright Gift	Deductible for income tax	No retained interest
Charitable Lead Trust	Allows property to transfer to heirs with little or no estate tax	No real income tax advantage
Pooled Income Fund	Deductible for income tax Variable income Managed by the charitable organization	Donor cannot be the trustee Not all charitable organizations are eligible
Charitable Remainder Unitrust	Deductible for income tax Avoids capital gains tax on appreciated property Variable income	May trigger alternative minimum tax Income will decline if the value of the fund declines
Charitable Remainder Annuity Trust	Deductible for income tax Avoids capital gains tax on appreciated property Fixed income	May trigger alternative minimum tax Income is fixed, regardless of need or inflation
Gift of Insurance	Deductible for income tax Enables donor to make large future gift at small cost	May require annual premiums

6

How CRT Distributions Are Taxed

While a Charitable Remainder Trust is tax exempt, its distributed income is considered taxable. Before outlining the alternative to this taxation, let's look at the Four-Tier System, which shows that income paid out to the beneficiary is taxed in the following priority order:

1. All current and undistributed ordinary income
2. All current and undistributed long-term capital gains
3. All current and undistributed tax-exempt income
4. Trust principal

With a CRUT or CRAT, the income payout must be made at least annually. If the trust's earnings are not sufficient to make the payout, the trustee (trust administrator) will be required to invade trust principal. The original principal always retains its income status, according to the Four-Tier System, as of the date the trust is established.

The key to preventing distribution of original principal is to select a payout rate that is lower than the anticipated earnings rate and administration fees. A fixed annuity with a long-term interest rate guarantee or a variable annuity that performs well in the early years can be used to reduce this risk. In essence, having defined an annuity as the investment inside of a CRT, two types of CRTs are being merged.

With that said, let's focus on taxation of income from the NIMCRUT (Net-Income-with-Make-Up) with an annuity:

First, remember that a NIMCRUT can only make an income distribution if the trust has generated earnings. If the trust principal is invested in an annuity contract, earnings are generated when the total value of the contract exceeds the total premiums paid into the contract. Therefore, annuity earnings distributed from the trust are always taxed as ordinary income.

Second, all earnings generated by a variable annuity are always taxed as ordinary income regardless of the investment inside the contract (stocks, bonds, etc.). Therefore, the trustee can participate in the equity and bond markets without being concerned about the type of income under the Four-Tier System.

In summary, a NIMCRUT funded with an annuity will always generate ordinary income. Thus, some of the complexities of the Four-Tier System are avoided and administration is made easier.

Why use a deferred annuity to fund a NIMCRUT?

Discovering the true significance of using a deferred annuity to fund a NIMCRUT requires closer examination. What

---

Trust Administrator

- Experience in CRTs essential
- Monitors taxes closely
- Intermediary among all the professionals

---

separates this type of strategy from other common investments is its benefits in income flexibility, security and simplicity.

Income Flexibility

Income flexibility is the primary benefit of funding the NIM-CRUT with an annuity. The key is that annuity income should be deferred for at least the first few years. This allows the annuity earnings to accumulate within the trust. Future financial objectives can then be accomplished by turning income "on" and "off." In other words, when the income is turned off, annuity earnings are accumulating. When it is turned on, income can be distributed.

Security

If the trustee wants to defer income, he has to invest in growth-oriented investments producing minimal income. These investments could be beyond the donor's risk tolerance level. When income is desired, the growth-oriented investments need to be changed to income-oriented investments. This could occur at an inopportune time and cause erosion of the trust principal. Also, these investments may not provide any death-benefit guarantee to the beneficiary (the charity).

The trustee should instead invest in an annuity instead of growth-oriented investments because:

1. Most clients are more comfortable with the risk level of an annuity compared to growth-only investments.
2. Trust principal is preserved since investment changes are not required to match income requirements.
3. Fixed annuity guarantees and the variable annuity guaranteed death benefits protect the remainder interest against market risk.

Simplicity

Since all annuity income is ordinary income, the trustee can make investment changes inside the annuity without being concerned about the type of income generated. But more importantly, trust administration is simplified since some of the complexities of the Four-Tier System are avoided.

Because NIMCRUTs are complex and require addressing several technical issues, it is recommended that a donor's attorney be involved in each phase of the drafting.

Precise language regarding "distributable trust income" must be included in this type of trust according to regulations under IRC 643(b) and state trust laws.

Treasury Regulation 1.664-3(b)(1) requires that the trust "income" be defined within the meaning of IRC 643(b). The code section defines "income" as whatever definition is provided in the governing trust instrument and applicable local/state law. Further, Treasury Regulation 1.643(b)-1 adds that any trust provisions which depart fundamentally from concepts of local law in the determination of what constitutes "income" are not recognized for federal tax purposes. Therefore, the trust's definition of trust "income" must not fundamentally depart from the state trust law definition of "distributable trust income."

Recognizing that the governing trust instrument must:
(a) provide for the inside build-up in the annuity to be considered income only when received by the trustee; and
(b) grant the trustee total discretion to decide when such amounts will be withdrawn from the annuity;
the trustee must be satisfied that these provisions are consistent with applicable state trust law.

Private Letter Ruling (PLR) 9009047 is the only PLR to date that has examined a NIMCRUT funded by a deferred annuity contract. Though the NIMCRUT was accepted as drafted, the issue of inside build-up as distributable trust income was not reviewed.

This copy of the PLR breaks down the specifics of the ruling and what it provides.

PRIVATE LETTER RULING 9009047
(CITATION — LR9009047)

Date: December 5, 1989

Refer Reply to: CC:P&SI:2 - TR-31-1430-89
LEGEND
A = ***
B = ***
W = ***
X = ***
Z = ***
Trustee = ***
Fund = ***

---

continued on the following page

Dear ***

This is in reply to your letter dated November 22, 1989, and prior to correspondence, written on behalf of X, requesting a ruling concerning the qualification of X as a charitable remainder unitrust under section 664(d)(2) of the Internal Revenue Code and the applicable regulations.

The information submitted states that X was executed on December 30, 1989, by A, B, and Trustee. A and B funded X with 600 shares of Y common stock. The Trustee proposes to invest the trust assets in a deferred annuity contract issued by Z.

Under the terms of the trust instrument, the Trustee shall pay to A and B, in equal shares during their lives, and then to the survivor for his or her life, in each tax year of X, an amount equal to the lesser of (a) the trust income for the tax year, or (b) seven and a half percent of the net fair market value of the trust assets valued as of the last day of such tax year. If the trust income in any tax year exceeds seven and a half percent of the net fair market value of the trust assets, the payment to A and B shall include such excess to the extent of any shortfall in prior years.

Upon the death of the survivor of A and B, all of the then principal and income of X shall be distributed to the Trustee to establish the Fund. The income credited to the Fund shall be used for the general purposes of W. If, at such time, W is not an organization described in section 170(b)(1)(A), 170(c), 2055(a), and 2522(a) of the Code, the Trustee will distribute the principal income of X to one or more organizations then so described as the Trustee shall select in his sole discretion.

The governing instrument as submitted with the request contains provisions set forth in Rev. Rul. 72-395, 1972-2 C.B.340, as modified by Rev. Rul. 80-123, 1980-1 C.B. 205, and Rev. Rul. 82-128, 1982-2 C.B. 71, clarified by Rev. Rul. 82-165, 1982-2 C.B. 117, as modified by Rev. Rul. 88-81, 1988—2 C.B. 127.

Section 664(d)(2) of the Code provides that for the purposes of section 664, a charitable remainder unitrust is a trust (A) from which a

continued on the following page

fixed percentage (not less than 5 percent) of the net fair market value of its assets, valued annually, is to be paid, not less often than annually, to one or more persons (at least one of which is not an organization described in section 170(c) and, in the case of individuals, only to an individual who is living at the time of creation of the trust) for a term of years (not in excess of 20 years) or for the life or the lives of such individual or individuals, (B) from which no amount other than the payments described in section 664(d)(2)(A) may be paid to or for the use of any person other than an organization described in section 170(c), and (C) following the termination of the payments described in section 664(d)(2)(A), the remainder interest in the trust is to be transferred to, or for the use of, an organization described in section 170(c) or is to be retained by the trust for such a use.

Section 664(D)(3) of the Code provides that notwithstanding the provisions of section 664(d)(2)(A) and (B), the trust instrument may provide that the trustee shall pay the income beneficiary for any year (A) the amount of the trust income, if such amount is less than the amount required to be distributed under section 664(d)(2)(A), and (B) any amount of the trust income which is in excess of the amount required to be distributed under section 664(d)(2)(A), to the extent that (by reason of section 664(d)(3)(A)) the aggregate of the amounts paid in prior years was less than the aggregate of such required amounts.

Section 72(u)(1) of the Code provides that if any annuity contract is held by a person who is not a natural person (A) such contract shall not be treated as an annuity contract for purposes of subtitle A (other than subchapter L) and (B) the income on the contract for any tax year of the policyholder shall be treated as ordinary income received or accrued by the owner during such tax year. For purposes of this paragraph, holding by a trust or other entity as an agent for a natural person shall not be taken into account.

Section 25.2512-6(a) of the Gift Tax Regulations provides, in part, that the value of a life insurance contract or of a contract for the payment of an annuity issued by a company regularly engaged in the selling of contracts of that character is established through the sale of the particular contract by the company, or through the sale by the company of comparable contracts.

continued on the following page

Section 20.2031-8(a)(1) of the Estate Tax Regulations provides, in part, that the value of a contract for the payment of an annuity, or an insurance policy on the life of a person other than the decedent, issued by a company regularly engaged in the selling of contracts of that character is established through the sale by that company of comparable contracts.

We conclude that the governing instrument will meet the requirements of a charitable remainder unitrust under section 664(d)(2) of the Code, provided the trust will be a valid trust under applicable state law.

Accordingly, X will qualify as a charitable remainder unitrust for federal income tax purposes for any year which it continues to meet the definition of the functions exclusively as a charitable remainder unitrust. For each year, X will be exempt from taxes imposed by subtitle A of the Code unless it has an unrelated business taxable income as defined in section 512 of the Code and the regulations applicable thereto.

X shall include in its ordinary income for any tax year the "income on the annuity contract" (within the meaning of section 72(u)(2) of the Code) because X will not hold the annuity contract as "an agent for a natural person" within the meaning of section 72(u)(1).

The annuity contract shall be valued at its "account value," i.e., the value on which interest earnings are computed, for purposes of determining the annual "net fair market value of the trust assets" under the terms of the trust instrument.

No opinion is expressed as to the federal tax consequences of the formation or operation of X under the provisions of any other section of the Code. No opinion is expressed as to any amendments to the provisions of X.

This ruling that X will qualify as a charitable remainder unitrust is subject to the condition that there are no changes in the law that would cause X to be disqualified.

continued on the following page

A copy of this letter should be attached to the federal tax return for the tax year X is established.

In accordance with the power of attorney on file, we are sending a copy of this letter to A and B.

This ruling letter is directed only to the taxpayer who requested it. Section 6110(j)(3) of the Code provides that it may not be used or cited as precedent.

Sincerely yours,

Claire E. Toth
Assistant to the Chief
Branch 2
Office of the Assistant
Chief Counsel
(Passthroughs and Special Industries)

Despite the complexities of the language, annuities are relatively easy to explain as opposed to other investments. People are more comfortable with an investment they understand. Annuities are also very easy to purchase and administer.

7

CRT Prospects

Having discussed the different types of Charitable Remainder Trusts and their popular uses, you've probably already developed a pretty good picture of those who would be considered a good prospect for a CRT.

Remember the older man in Florida who wanted to give his New Jersey property to his local church? How about the doctor who was looking to get the most out of selling his practice, or the man who discovered an opportune way to support his alma mater while securing his daughter's continued education?

If you look at them individually, these people may seem quite different. They surely vary in their interests, even their outlook on life. But if you look closer, these people, and others to be mentioned, share objectives very important to them. Whether looking to protect or enhance their own financial well-being or that of a charity close to their heart, they all found a means to their end in the Charitable Remainder Trust.

Who Can Donate?

- Individuals
- Corporations
- Partnerships
- Trusts

While not always the case, the primary characteristic of a CRT prospect is one who possesses "Charitable Receptivity." Charitable Receptivity is just as it sounds, one who is receptive to charitable giving.

This type of person either has a history of some sort of charitable giving or has expressed an interest in learning more about how they can help.

As we discussed earlier, most people who contribute to a nonprofit organization are aware of the tax deduction that comes with such a donation. Whether it be an individual or corporation, financial or in-kind gifts are usually made annually at a time that is financially convenient to the donor. The timing of their gifts also tend to come at the end of each year, in time to declare their gift on their next tax return.

But CRT prospects also exhibit other interests in their charitable planning. They are often trying to achieve any of the following:

- Avoid capital gains tax on the sale of a highly appreciated asset
- Increase current or future income
- Reduce current income taxes
- Establish future income for surviving spouse
- Reduce estate taxes
- Conserve estate for heirs
- Build a retirement and/or college fund

Are You a Candidate for a CRT?

- Expectant retiree
- Holder of large stock/bond portfolio
- Executive with highly appreciated stock
- Real estate/land owner
- Closely held business owner wanting to sell
- Wealthy individual wanting to maximize benefits to heirs

Of course, many people at the outset may look to a CRT simply for financial reasons, and others may be considering a CRT strictly for charitable reasons.

The example involving the man worried about his daughter's college pursuits demonstrated the notion that most people do possess a charitable interest of some sort, even if they may not realize it at first. Strong ties with a college, church, local youth group or other private or public charity always makes for a stronger CRT prospect.

Those looking to offer assets or a gift to a charitable cause find the idea of the CRT all the more attractive when they learn the benefits that come with it. These are people who tend to give to charity because they want to make a difference, to make their mark in life, to leave a legacy.

Many times individuals, and even corporations, give to specific nonprofit organizations for simpler reasons; they might know someone who works there, volunteers there, or just read about the organization in the newspaper or heard something about it on the news.

Other times, they give because their mother or father used to make a donation to a particular nonprofit. Before they know it, the organization considers them loyal and reli-

---

Why a Charitable Remainder Trust?

- You desire to maximize cash flow from highly appreciated assets
- You are concerned about taxes
- You prefer "voluntary" philanthropy

---

able contributors, even if there is little contact with them. These are the types of people who might make for good CRT prospects, those who have yet to learn what more their contributions could be doing for themselves, their heirs and the charity.

Most charities have a planned giving department or development director who work on their own and with planned giving specialists to seek out CRT prospects of all kinds.

Psychological Profile

Having touched on some of the different reasons people give to charity, it might serve our marketing objectives to delve further into those reasons, specifically centering on those who wish to leave a mark or legacy.

In an article first published by the *Journal of the American Society of CLU & ChFC* (Volume XLI, No. 2), Mark S. Dorfman, PhD, and Charles P. Flynn, PhD, examine the psychological motivations that perhaps drive our need to leave something behind.

The article, "Immortality-Striving, Heroism, and Power: Psychological Contributions to Life Insurance Marketing," revisits the work of Earnest Becker, whose contributions to the literature of psychology in the early 1900s included the book *The Denial of Death*, which earned him a posthumous Pulitzer Prize. Dorfman and Flynn apply Becker's theories of human motivation to the marketing methods of today's life insurance professionals, which also pertains to those marketing Charitable Remainder Trusts.

"Becker's central theme," the authors write, "was that much human striving (and strife) could be attributed to the struggle against the foreknowledge of death."

They assert that Becker saw humans as having an inability to grasp our own mortality, and that this obsession is tied to our constant search for purpose and meaning in life. Becker's notion, according to the authors, is that our motivation to leave something behind is, in essence, an attempt to overcome the limits of our own existence.

Because we are so keenly aware of our mortality, the authors assert Becker's claim that we crave some continuity beyond our life. They define this craving as "immortality-striving."

The authors then go on to suggest that "life insurance can and should be perceived as one particular kind of immortality vehicle." Charitable Remainder Trusts are, of course, one form of life insurance.

The upshot is that our need as humans to strive for some assurance that our life has counted, has had an impact, in some heroic way, includes the act of leaving something behind for others.

This, within the model of "immortality-striving" and Becker's theory, is in some measure a "form of victory over death."

"The purchase of sufficient life insurance," the writers continue, "allows the individual to gain a sense of heroic status in the lives of the beneficiaries he or she continues to affect." He or she will be remembered and, in effect, immortalized.

Becker's theory holds that while we as humans strive toward this level of immortality after death, we are also consumed with achieving a similar kind of heroism and power while alive. This is how we measure our self-worth and, perhaps, how we attain our self-esteem.

From Becker's view of our human motivations, Dorfman and Flynn conclude that his theories suggest successful life insurance marketing hinges on satisfying those human needs: "the need to make a heroic action, to achieve a kind of immortality, and the need to accumulate and exercise power during one's life."

This, they write, translates into marketing approaches "emphasizing the lasting good an insured can do by purchasing life insurance, the continuing influence the individual may exercise through this purchase, and the turning of the defeat of death into a financial victory benefiting one's family."

The same is true in marketing the Charitable Remainder Trust. In fact, the CRT goes one further in Becker's prognosis of human motivations. Not only does a CRT provide and enhance income for the donor today and secure the financial future of his or her heirs tomorrow, but the CRT provides the opportunity for the donor to support a charitable organization today and tomorrow.

The CRT, in essence, is its own marketing tool. The key to its continued growth in popularity is in articulating those benefits and applying them to the natural human motivations Becker detailed years ago. The CRT is not just an investment in the future, it's a plan for the present.

8

Finding the Best Prospects

If you were to subscribe to Earnest Becker's psychological profile of mankind, you could say the search for the best prospects for the CRT begins at home. It's safe to say that we all strive for the freedom that financial stability affords us, especially because it also often affords us the ability to take care of others.

In the previous chapters we have been able to reveal a number of characteristics of CRT prospects, and we have discovered that they are not always as similar as we might have guessed. But we have been able to narrow down a few things about our best CRT prospects, which helps in discovering where we might find them:

- Those looking, planning, or currently living in retirement are among the most viable candidates to benefit from the CRT. Many retirees take time to research the opportunities and options of leaving gifts and/or assets to their heirs and/or favorite charities.

"Baby Busters"
Ages 51 to 65

- Inadequate planning-to-date
  - Social security uncertain
  - Know impact of inflation
  - Fearful of markets
  - Victims of tax reform
- Most will be 65 by the year 2000
- Control most of the non-corporate assets in the U.S.

Source: Statistical Abstract of the United States 1993

- Those planning for future support of a spouse through a Will are likely to consider the benefits and advantages of establishing a CRT.
- Those looking to reduce taxes in real estate, income or other assets will find more secure advantages in the CRT.
- Those with children approaching college age are looking for options that allow them to afford tuition costs. The CRT is a unique and effective option they may not have considered — until now.
- Those who wish to leave their wealth to a charitable organization of their choice with money that would more likely go toward taxes.
- Those who own a highly appreciated asset and wish to maximize its wealth potential.

The best prospects with the best assets make for the perfect use of the CRT. The most desirable assets to transfer to a CRT have a low-cost basis, produce a minimal income,

"Baby Boomers" Ages 30 to 50

- Many plan to retire before age 60
- Most know social security and pensions are insufficient for comfortable living
- Contemporary families
  - Dual income
  - Single parent
- Entering their peak earning years

Source: Statistical Abstract of the United States 1993

are debt-free and are able to be sold. Let's look at the best and worst assets:

BEST
- Cash
- Publicly traded securities
- Real estate (debt-free)

WORST
- Debt-encumbered real estate
- Personal property with unrelated charitable use
- Businesses (not being sold)

Assets Ideal for CRTs

- Real estate
- Stock
- Small business

The typical transaction involves either highly appreciated publicly traded stock or real estate, but it is important to remember that the asset cannot be sold or have a sale pending before the CRT is established.

By creating some real-life planning situations, we can illustrate just how assets are transferred to a CRT and the projected outcome of such a transaction.

Retiring Employee with Substantial Company Stock (or, Too Many Eggs in One Basket, Must Diversify)

Let's say there's a potential donor heavily involved in her company's stock purchase program or incentive stock option program and finds herself with 25% to 60% of total net worth in the stock of one issuer — the employer.

Now, with 30 years or more of retirement ahead, she is nervous about the lack of diversification and wishes to reinvest. But because of her conservative nature, she is certain she wants to reinvest in something that is risk-adverse and fairly stable. However, her holdings have appreciated substantially over a long holding period, and based on current share values, income taxes will severely erode the portfolio.

On the other hand, to avoid income taxes these shares could be transferred to a Charitable Remainder Trust and sold. The proceeds could then be reinvested in a diversified portfolio without taxation by the trustee, and she could enjoy the peace of mind that comes with a regular check in the mail for the rest of her life.

Jack & Beth Armstrong

- $600,000 of common stock
- Gift from Beth's father
- Low-cost basis
- Paying 2% dividends yearly
- Want to increase income

Solution #1

Sell the stocks — reinvest

$600,000	×	2%	=	$12,000
	−	33%		(combined federal and state
[200,000]				capital gains tax rates)
$400,000	×	7%	=	$28,000

Result: Increase income, *pay* $200,000 to IRS!

Hypothetical investment only. Not meant to represent performance of actual investment.

Solution #2

Establish a CRT
Transfer stock to CRT
Sell stock capital gains tax free

$600,000	×	2%	=	$12,000
		0%		(combined federal and state
				capital gains tax rates)
$600,000	×	7%	=	$42,000

Result: Triple the income with *no* capital gains tax!

Hypothetical investment only. Not meant to represent performance of actual investment.

Retiree with Unimproved Real Estate or Industrial Stocks (or, Looks Good in a Balance Sheet but Lousy Income)

This is a classic case for a Charitable Remainder Trust. A man reaching his retirement age has held a parcel of raw land and a portfolio of industrial stocks for long-term growth during his working years, and now he wishes to reposition for maximum income. The land produces no income. The industrial stocks yield 2.4% on average. Let's trade for 9% AA rated bonds. But wait! The land and stock have tripled in value over the years, and federal and state income taxes will claim 35% of growth if he repositions.

A Charitable Remainder Trust could reposition the assets without paying a capital gains tax and payout 6% or 7% of current market value of assets.

Funding the "Benefit Blackout Period" (or, The Early Retirement)

There's a successful executive or investor who is 45 to 55 years of age and wants to play more golf, travel, etc. The problem is that Mr. Fastrack won't be eligible for Social Security retirement benefits until age 62, and his company retirement program is geared to pay benefits at age 60 for early retirees.

Further, his IRA account, while accessible before age 59½, offers little flexibility of payment scheduled before that time.

In the words of Rod Serling, "Welcome, my friends, to the Twilight Zone." Or, in this case, the "benefit blackout period."

Case Study — Small Business

The Gilbert Brothers

- Own a small software company
- $12 million market value
- Low-cost basis

Solution #1

Sell company — reinvest
$12,000,000

– 33%		(combined federal and state
[4,000,000]		capital gains tax rates)

$8,000,000 × 7% = $560,000

Hypothetical investment only. Not meant to represent performance of actual investment.

Solution #2

Establish a CRT
Transfer business ownership to CRT
Sell business capital gains tax free
$12,000,000

– 0%		(combined federal and state
		capital gains tax rates)

$12,000,000 × 7% = $840,000

Result: Increase supplemental retirement income with *no* capital gains tax!

Hypothetical investment only. Not meant to represent performance of actual investment.

Mr. Fastrack intends to do some consulting, but there is still shortfall of income to provide the desired lifestyle. Enter the "Term of Years" Charitable Remainder Trust. To supplement the 7- or 10-year period before regular retirement benefits flow, he contributes land, securities, etc., to a 7- to 10-year Charitable Remainder Trust with a high payout rate of 10% to 12%.

Preserving the Large Estate (or, Liquefying "Horses and Ham")

Show me a person who paid $5 million in federal estate tax and I'll show you a person whose total net worth exceeded $10 million and 90% of it was represented by a business interest or real estate holdings.

This is the classic case of the large estate owner who is cash poor and inventory rich. Sure, she could make lifetime gifts, buy life insurance in an irrevocable trust among other things, but all she has is horses and hams. You can't pay life insurance premiums with capital assets.

Here the donor can save from 50% to 60% shrinkage of the estate by converting some of those capital assets into income on a tax-favored basis, and then buy all the third-party owner life insurance that the cash flow allows. Yes, the Charitable Remainder Unitrust or Annuity Trust provides the vehicle to create this miracle.

Blessed is the Landlord (or, For He Shall Grow Tired of Tenants)

Forty years ago, a couple bought their first rental property —- a duplex. They managed it. When tenants left, they cleaned it, painted it, repaired it, advertised it, and rented it. It grew in value; their cost basis depreciated. Selling meant declaring a large taxable gain, so upon the advice of their CPA, they made a tax-deferred exchange instead for four units. Their CPA, by the way, never managed rentals.

Now the couple managed four units for a year or two. History repeated itself and they exchanged the four units for eight units. They managed these for a year or two and the routine continued.

Flash forward 40 years. Their CPA looks young, plays golf. The couple looks old, manages 80 units and, while they hired a full-time property manager years ago, somehow they cannot insulate themselves from the hassle.

The couple has reached the age of reflection. They desire freedom from asset management, a lifetime income, a tax-wise estate plan, peace and tranquility.

They visit their CPA. He starts to say the word "exchange," but the look on their faces tells him he'd better have a better idea. When he tells them about the Charitable Remainder Trust, they discover an opportunity they wish he had mentioned years before.

Minimizing the Bit on those "Minimum" Withdrawals (or, IRS Ultimately Takes 60% to 70%)

Since IRA accumulations ultimately account for every tax known to civilized man, affluent donors are often advised to take the full $150,000 per year allowed without triggering the excise tax and spending it, making cash gifts to heirs or to buy life insurance owned by a third party. However, many

Case Study — Real Property

Mr. and Mrs. Wells (retired)

- Own real property
- $1.5 million market value
- Highly appreciated
- Want to provide for children and heirs

Solution #1

Sell real property — reinvest

$1,500,000	– 33%	(combined federal and state
[500,000]		capital gains tax rates)
$1,000,000	× 7% =	$70,000

Result: *No* estate planning benefits.

Hypothetical investment only. Not meant to represent performance of actual investment.

Solution #2

Establish a CRT
Transfer property to CRT
Sell property capital gains tax free

$1,500,000	– 0%	(combined federal and state
		capital gains tax rates)
$1,500,000	× 7% =	$105,000

Result: (1) Increase retirement income with *no* capital gains tax! (2) Tax deduction funds life policy as wealth replacement.

Hypothetical investment only. Not meant to represent performance of actual investment.

middle income people take the minimum required age at 71 and beyond, seeking to preserve their nest egg.

Take the 74-year-old man with $70,000 of other retirement income whose minimum IRA withdrawal this year is $38,000. Considering federal and state tax, 40% of this is going to be confiscated. Now, if the man took about $25,000 of this cash and contributed it to a Charitable Gift Annuity, the income tax deduction would be available up to 50% of adjusted gross income and, at age 74, he is guaranteed 7.5% for his lifetime. This is a great way to cut the effective tax rate from 40% to 26%, while bolstering his income.

We talked about the advantages of a CRT in terms of a small business. Through various applications, a business owner is able to increase the value of that business and avoid being taxed on the sale of the business.

As we said, the sale of a business often accounts for much of the owner's retirement income. But this type of saving can also be increased through a supplemental pension plan. The sole purpose of plans like a 401K, IRA and Keogh among others is to provide you with retirement income.

The Charitable Remainder Trust does this and more. No other vehicle affords you a tax deduction every time you fund a non-qualified plan. You get a tax deductible contribution, tax-deferred growth (if funded with an annuity through NIMCRUT), unlimited contributions, access to funds prior to age 59½ without IRS penalties, and lifetime income.

Corporate stock options are another avenue in putting a CRT to work for your retirement income. How many employees have stock options that may be exercised at a discount to fair market value, but they don't necessarily want to incur an additional tax liability? How many corporations host annual capital campaigns for charities?

This is a tremendous opportunity to create a cause marketing opportunity for all involved. Market the CRT to fulfill

Why a Charitable Remainder Trust for You?

- Creates a source of lifetime income to supplement retirement
- Enhances use of highly appreciated assets
- Avoids capital gains and estate taxation
- Tax-free compounding
- Makes significant future charitable gift
- Increases inheritance to your heirs (wealth replacement)

a cause (the charity), the employee benefits because he now frees up an asset without tax liability, locks in the gain, gets a tax deduction, and now can reinvest the proceeds into a more diversified portfolio that looks out for his future.

9

Identifying a Charity

It's no secret why charitable organizations receive the bulk of their contributions at the end of each year. For both individuals and corporations, charitable gifts mean tax deductions and the end of each year is the deadline to include such write-offs on their next return.

For those with a Planned Giving Arrangement, this deadline is less significant because a strategy has been set in motion. Through planned giving, there is no annual search for charitable organizations that would reward the donor a tax deduction and, in applying the proper plan, annual contributions become much more than a simple write-off.

It is in this way that the Charitable Remainder Trust is not just a sophisticated tax avoidance, a savvy investment and a generous donation rolled into one. As Earnest Becker might contend, this type of trust is an exercise in control that continues from beyond the grave.

Through a Planned Giving Arrangement that includes all the multi-faceted advantages of a Charitable Remainder

Why Give to Charity through a CRT?

- Need income
- Want to avoid capital gains tax
- Want tax deductions
- Wish to diversify without triggering tax
- Want assets beyond creditors' reach
- Desire to choose charitable beneficiaries
- Need to control investment decisions

Trust, a long-term relationship is forged between the donor and the charity closest to the donor's heart.

Smart donors, however, should not be content with their emotional support of an organization's mission. In a Planned Giving Arrangement, donors should take time to learn more about how the charity operates. Getting to know the organization from a business standpoint helps a donor realize how their contribution is being or will be spent.

By determining what percentage of a charity's budget goes to their actual cause rather than back into fund-raising initiatives, administrative costs, travel expenses, etc., donors get a better picture whether their contribution is making the type of impact they desire.

While nonprofits in their first few years of existence may have some reason for high administrative costs, those with a consistently unbalanced distribution of income should be avoided.

Before getting this far, however, donors should make sure that organization(s) they intend to donate to qualify under IRS tax-approved status. Donors should be skeptical of those that pitch their financial muscle as a way to increase

Who Gives to Charity?

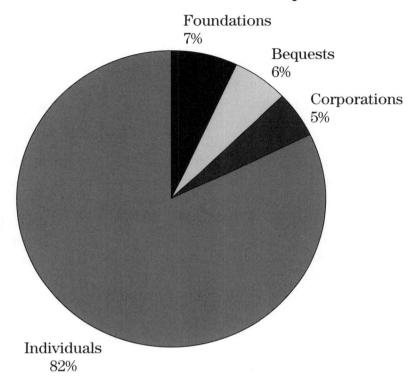

Foundations
7%

Bequests
6%

Corporations
5%

Individuals
82%

Source: The Chronicle of Philanthropy, *June 1, 1993*

investment returns. It is also unwise to blindly donate to a charity through phone or mail solicitations.

Marketing to charities

While charitable organizations are always in search of new fund-raising ideas and opportunities, they are often wary of approaches with which they are unfamiliar. Because competition for a limited amount of dollars is growing even more fierce, nonprofits tend to be sensitive about their donor base and who they allow into their sphere of influence.

Those marketing to such organizations should proceed with caution when introducing a concept like the Charitable Remainder Trust. In gaining an audience with a leader or leaders of nonprofits, you should begin by contacting the director of development or foundation director by letter or phone. It might serve your purposes well to offer a brief synopsis of how the Charitable Remainder Trust can help their organization and an example that illustrates how it works.

At the outset, you should also dispel any concerns they might have about your own intentions, about why you want to help them. Give them the "what's in it for you." Be open and honest: simply tell them you have the resources and expertise they may not have, and they have access to donors and assets you don't have. Tell them that if you can raise hundreds of thousands of dollars for the charity, all you want in return is to help manage the money you raise. Sounds reasonable, doesn't it?

Charities are often willing to listen to and learn about an idea that makes sense. If you show them how you can help couple philanthropy with economic benefit to their donors, they are likely to agree to a meeting where you can outline this concept in more detail.

I think you'll experience what I have. After providing them the basics on the CRT, the guard comes down and the foundation director is led into a dialogue on the possibilities.

My greatest experience has been working with the 1996 Atlanta Paralympic Games. This nonprofit organization is made up of physically challenged athletes (paraplegics, quadreplegics, and athletes with cerebral palsy) competing in Olympic games much like the regular Olympics. Having helped establish this organization's planned giving center

Eligible Nonprofits

- Museums
- Hospitals
- Schools
- Churches

based in Washington, D.C., I've seen first-hand the enthusiasm with which nonprofit leaders have embraced the opportunities of the Charitable Remainder Trust.

I have also been enlightened by the way the leaders of this charity give so much of themselves. When they ask others to give, it's merely an extension of their personality. They are passionate in their cause and are not shy about asking for help. They realize that people will not always give away sizable assets if they feel it's going to jeopardize their financial well-being. They know you have to demonstrate the ways in which their gift counts. And with the CRT, the leaders of these types of organizations have also been able to show how donors can enhance their own finances through giving.

Still, as we have seen, CRTs are a sophisticated form of planned giving. In most cases, a trust attorney needs to be in place to draft the trust properly with administration being handled by a qualified professional or an organization like Renaissance Inc., which is America's leading charitable gift planning consultant, administrator and facilitator.

But this team approach in providing the resources and tools to establish and monitor a CRT is just another strength in the marketing strategy.

Marketing the Charitable Remainder Trust to nonprofit organizations like the 1996 Atlanta Paralympic Games also opens doors to major corporations. Entry into this often in-accessible market is made easier through a cause marketing campaign.

A cause marketing campaign is much like a corporate sponsorship where both the charity and the corporation band together to help each other. The end result is further expo-sure and financial reward for both parties.

The work American Express has done with Easter Seals in the past serves as a good example of a cause marketing campaign, where a portion of the proceeds of American Ex-press sales were donated to the Easter Seals.

Coca-Cola has worked with the Olympics, when a per-centage of their sales funded Olympic events. With a cause marketing approach, you are able to solicit a cause and are provided a venue for your own product that should have a di-rect impact on your sales and business growth. Contribu-tions to the charity are tax-deductible.

The work of the John Hancock Company as well as ITT Hartford with both the regular and Special Olympics has al-ready proven a success. Since beginning their sponsorship in 1993, agents of the company have hosted over 250 events.

Speaking engagements at sporting events and associa-tion meetings alone have provided more than 3,000 leads. One agent alone received 700 leads after setting up a booth at a gymnastics meet. He attributed $125,000 in commissions directly to his involvement.

With this type of marketing strategy, company repre-sentatives are able to represent a cause, mixing an emotion-al appeal with their own marketing plan.

A cause marketing campaign allows organizations like the 1996 Atlanta Paralympics, a charity without the resources and sex appeal to draw major corporate sponsors, to gener-ate a plan that gives corporations a double-barreled reason to

Types of Charities

- Tax-exempt vs. tax-exempt and tax-deductible
- Public vs. private
- Endowed vs. currently supported

become a partner. This is simply another example of coupling philanthropy and economic benefit.

Many charitable organizations have taken to the internet to promote their good work and search for donors. Some have even used the information superhighway to suggest a variety of ways individuals, corporations or private foundations can help their cause.

Columbia University of New York is among the many institutions that outlines in specific detail the advantages to making planned gifts through pooled income funds and charitable remainder unitrusts and annuities. The school's home page also includes a phone number and address for browsers who would like to request more information.

Through their online outlet, the University of Kansas recently announced a local couple's gift of a charitable remainder unitrust valued at $47,500 to its School of Medicine. They also used the forum to recognize the donors, explain how the unitrust was established and how it can help in the school's education and research.

This type of promotion is not limited to educational institutions. Smaller nonprofits are getting in on the internet act as are a diverse number of specialized causes.

The Hindu Heritage Endowment (HHE) can be found online hailing the Charitable Remainder Trust and how it can help their cause of aiding Hindu institutions dedicated to traditional and classical Hindu principles and practices.

This organization even includes an example of how such a gift might work for them.

Prakash Singh, age 55, is a successful computer engineer who owns 10,000 shares of company stock worth $30 a share. He wants to eventually donate this to HHE to establish an endowment in his own and his wife's name to benefit a nearby temple they attend regularly. Prakash also needs to use this stock, which is yielding ½%, to create additional income for his retirement years. In consultation with his estate planner, a charitable remainder 6% unitrust is created and the stock is placed into it, sold and higher yielding investments are purchased.

Prakash receives a $100,000 charitable deduction. This amount is determined by the $300,000 amount transferred to the Charitable Remainder Trust, his age of 55 and the yearly life income of 6%. This deduction lowers his income tax by $39,600 (39.6% of the $100,000 deduction).

Through the use of a Charitable Remainder Trust, Prakash avoids the capital gains tax of $84,000 (28% of the gain of $300,000). Thus the amount available to reinvest is $300,000, and the initial 6% income is $18,000 a year. If Prakash sold the stock he would pay the capital gains tax, which would reduce the amount available to reinvest to $216,000 and the initial 6% income to $12,960 a year. By using the trust, Prakash increases his income by 39%.

The size of the gift eventually placed in his and his wife's name will also be 39% greater. For example, if Prakash passes on at age 80, the $300,000 in the trust could appreciate through prudent investment over the 25-year period to $628,000, while without a trust the $216,000 could appreciate to $452,000.

There are many different types of organizations engaged in a variety of charitable, religious, educational and other activities. They are often referred to collectively as charitable organizations, but this general term is not entirely accurate in determining whether a donor will receive the tax results anticipated from a charitable gift to a specific organization.

The terms "charitable organization" and "exempt organization" are not synonymous. The term charitable organization is generally used to describe an organization to which gifts are deductible for income, gift or estate tax purposes.

The term exempt organization is used to describe any organization that is exempt from federal income tax. Although many types of organizations are exempt from income tax, the charitable contribution deduction is available only for gifts or bequests to a select group.

It is important for a donor to know for certain where an organization stands under the law because gifts to some organizations may qualify for a particular charitable deduction, while gifts to others may not; because gifts to certain organizations may qualify for the maximum income tax charitable deduction, while gifts to others may not; and because the classification of the donee under the tax law may determine whether the donor is allowed an income tax deduction for the full value of the gift.

The IRS publishes a book called Publication 78 — often referred to as "The Cumulative List" or "The Blue Book" — to remove any uncertainty as to the deductibility of a gift. The book lists all organizations qualified to receive gifts for which an income tax charitable deduction is allowable. It can also, for the most part, be used to confirm the deductibility of payments for gift and estate tax purposes.

If an organization does not appear in Publication 78, it does not necessarily mean that contributions to the organization are not deductible. Some organizations may be listed under a parent organization or the organization may not have made the most revised edition. The book is updated annually as of October 31.

However, if an organization is not listed a donor should request a copy of its determination letter and written assurance that it is still effective and under what terms.

10

Setting Up a CRT

Most donors have at least charitable intent. To successfully bring the charitable gift to fruition, that charitable intent must surface and be expressed throughout the entire process.

Here, in brief outline, are the steps the donor and CRT team take in bringing the agreement from the idea stage to full implementation.

1. Identify the donor's (or prospect's) opportunity:
   - Suitable asset
   - Estate and income tax issues
   - Willingness to transfer asset
   - Charitable intent
2. Help the donor understand the benefits of a Charitable Remainder Trust:
   - To the donor
   - To the family
   - To the community

3. Gather information on the needs of the donor.
   Good information is critical to good case design.
4. Design the case.
   Critical to meeting the donor's objectives.
5. Present the completed design.
   Important to keep it simple and concise.
6. Once the donor is committed, assemble the donor's team, which may include:
   - Attorney
   - Accountant
   - Money manager(s)
   - Heirs
   - Designated charitable organization(s)
7. Deal with questions and objections with the help of the CRT team.
8. Have the preparation of the donor's trust document done by an estate planning attorney well versed in CRTs.
9. On behalf of the donor, apply for necessary insurance.
10. Implement the trust:
    - Execute the final trust documents
    - Transfer the asset to the trust
    - Sell the asset and reinvest for diversification
    - Help the donor define a money management philosophy
11. Give the donor's team a lasting impression of your professionalism:
    - Create a donor binder
    - Ongoing evaluation and monitoring of gift performance
    - Donor recognition (e.g., dinner with donor and charity, etc.)

Drafting a CRT

While the actual drafting of a CRT is usually left to a trust attorney, it is important to be familiar with the characteristics of such an agreement. Below is a sample of a basic charitable remainder unitrust with one donor.

SPECIMEN AGREEMENT

Charitable Remainder Unitrust
One Life—Plan '1'

UNITRUST AGREEMENT made this day of May 1, 1996, between JOHN DOE, residing at 11 First Street, Chicago, Illinois, (hereinafter called the "Donor") and XYZ University, an Illinois educational corporation located in Chicago, Illinois (hereinafter called the "Trustee").

1. The Donor transfers and delivers to the Trustee the property described in the annexed Schedule "A." This property and all receipts of every kind shall be managed and invested by the Trustee as a single fund (hereinafter called the "unitrust").

2. (A) The Trustee shall pay to the Donor (in cash, in kind, or partly in each) in each taxable year of the unitrust during his life trust a unitrust amount equal to five percent (5%) of the net fair market value of the trust assets valued as of the first day of each taxable year of the unitrust (decreased as provided in paragraph 2(B)

---

in the case where the taxable year is a short taxable year or is the taxable year in which the Donor dies and increased as provided in paragraph 2(C) in the case where there are additional contributions in the taxable year). The unitrust amount shall be paid in equal quarterly installments (on the last day of March, June, September and December, with the first installment to be on the last day of the month of _____, 19??) from income and, to the extent income is insufficient, from principal. Any income of the unitrust for a taxable year in excess of the unitrust amount shall be added to principal. Notwithstanding any existing or hereafter enacted state law, no amount other than the unitrust amount may be paid to or for the use of any person other than an organization described in each of section 170(b)(1)(A), section 170(c), section 2055(a) and section 2522(a) of the Internal Revenue Code of 1996 (hereinafter called the "Code"). However, an amount shall not be deemed to be paid to or for the use of any person other than an organization described in the aforesaid Code sections if the amount is transferred for full and adequate consideration.

(B) The first taxable year of the unitrust begins with the date of this Agreement and shall end on December 31, 19??. Subsequent taxable years shall be on a calendar year basis. In the case of a taxable year which is for a period of less than 12 months (other than the taxable year in which the Donor dies), the unitrust amount which must be distributed under paragraph 2(A) shall be such amount multiplied by a fraction the numerator of which is the number of days in the taxable year of the unitrust and the denominator of which is 365 (366 if February 29 is a day included in the numerator). In the case of the taxable year in which the Donor dies, the unitrust amount which must be distributed under paragraph 2(A) shall be such amount multiplied by a fraction the numerator of which is the number of days in the period beginning on the first day of such taxable year and ending on the date of the Donor's death and the denominator of which is 365 (366 if February 29 is a day included in the numerator). Notwithstanding the foregoing, the obligation of the Trustee to pay the unitrust amount shall terminate with the regular quarterly installment next proceeding the Donor's death.

(C) The Donor and others may, from time to time, add property acceptable to the Trustee to the unitrust.

(1) If any additional contributions are made to the unitrust after the initial contribution in trust, the unitrust amount for the taxable year in which the assets are added to the trust shall be five percent (5%) of the sum of (a) the net fair market value of the trust assets (excluding the assets so added and any income from, or appreciation on, such assets), and (b) that proportion of the value of the assets so added that was excluded under (a) which the

number of days in the period which begins with the date of contribution and ends with the earlier of the last day of the taxable year or the Donor's death bears to the number of days in the period which begins on the first day of such taxable year ends with the earlier of the last day in such taxable year or the Donor's death. The assets so added shall be valued at the time of the contribution.

(2) If any additional contribution is made by Will, the obligation to pay the unitrust amount with respect to such additional contribution shall commence with the date of death of the person under whose Will the additional contribution is made, but payment of such unitrust amount may be deferred from such date of death to the end of the taxable year of the unitrust in which occurs the complete funding of the additional contribution. Within a reasonable period after such time, the Trustee shall pay, in the case of an underpayment, or shall receive from the Donor, in the case of an overpayment, the difference between any unitrust amounts actually paid to the Donor, plus interest on such amounts computed at the rate of interest prescribed in the Federal Income Tax Regulations (Treasury Regulations) under section 664 of the Code, compounded annually, and the unitrust amounts payable, plus interest on such amounts computed

at the rate of interest prescribed in the Treasury Regulations under section 664 of the Code, compounded annually. The unitrust amounts payable shall be retroactively determined by using the unitrust's taxable year, valuation method and valuation date and following the rules specified in section 1.664-1(a)(5)(i) of the Treasury Regulations.

(D) If the net fair market value of the unitrust assets is incorrectly determined by the Trustee for any taxable year, then within a reasonable period after the final determination of the correct value, the Trustee shall pay to the Donor in the case of an undervaluation or shall receive from the Donor in the case of an overvaluation an amount equal to the difference between the unitrust amount properly payable and the unitrust amount actually paid.

(E) Upon the Donor's death, the Trustee shall distribute all of the then principal and income of the unitrust, other than any amount due to the Donor, to XYZ University for its general purposes. If XYZ University is not an organization described in each of section 170(b)(1)(A), section 170(c), section 2055(a) and section 2522(a) of the Code at the time when any principal or income of the unitrust is distributed to it, the Trustee shall distribute such principal or income to one or more organizations then so described as the Trustee shall select in its sole discretion and in such shares as it shall determine.

3. In computing the net fair market value of the unitrust assets there shall be taken into account all assets and liabilities without regard to whether particular items are taken into account in determining the income of the unitrust. All determinations of the unitrust's fair market value shall be in accordance with generally accepted fiduciary accounting principles and any United States Treasury requirements governing charitable remainder unitrusts. In any conflict Treasury requirements shall prevail over generally accepted fiduciary accounting principles and any inconsistent provisions of this Agreement.

4. In addition to the powers conferred upon it by law, the Trustee is authorized to retain the property described in Schedule "A," or may sell the property, invest and reinvest the unitrust in any kind of property, without diversification as to kind or amount and without regard to the limitations imposed by law on investments, except that it may not invest in assets which do not have an objective, ascertainable market value, such as real estate or stock in a closely held corporation. Nothing in this Agreement shall be construed to restrict the Trustee from investing the unitrust assets in a manner which could result in the annual realization of a reasonable amount of income or gain from the sale or disposition of trust assets.

5. The Trustee shall not receive compensation for services rendered under this Agreement. No bond or other security shall be required of the Trustee in any jurisdiction.

6. In creating this unitrust, Donor intends to obtain the full benefit of any income, gift and estate tax

charitable deductions to which he (and his estate) may be entitled under the Code and for the unitrust to qualify as a charitable remainder unitrust under section 664 of the Code and the regulations thereunder. Accordingly, this unitrust shall be interpreted, valued, managed, invested, administered and in all other respects governed consistent with the Donor's intent. Without limiting the generality of the foregoing, the Trustee is prohibited (except for the payment of the unitrust amount to the Donor) from engaging in any act of self-dealings as defined in section 4941(d) of the Code, from retaining any excess business holdings as defined in section 4943(c) of the Code which would subject the unitrust to tax under section 4943 of the Code, from making any investments which would subject the unitrust to tax under section 4944 of the Code, and from making any taxable expenditures as defined in section 4945(d) of the Code. If section 4942 of the Code is deemed applicable to the unitrust by reason of section 508(e) of the Code or otherwise, the Trustee shall make distributions at such time and in such a manner as not to subject the unitrust to tax under section 4942 of the Code.

7. No federal estate taxes, state death taxes or any other estate, death or inheritance taxes ("death taxes") regarding the unitrust shall be allocated to or be recoverable from the unitrust. The Donor imposes an obligation on his estate to pay any death taxes from sources other than the unitrust and agrees to so provide in his Will or in another way. This provision may be enforced by XYZ University in its capacity as trustee, charitable remainderman, or both.

8. This Agreement is irrevocable.

9. The Trustee shall have the power to amend this Agreement for the sole purpose of complying with the requirements of section 664 of the Code and Treasury Regulations sections 1.664-1 and 1.664-3.

10. This Agreement is made pursuant to, and shall be interpreted in accordance with, the laws of the State of Illinois. However, in any conflict with section 664 of the Code, the regulations thereunder or any other existing or hereafter promulgated legislative or Treasury requirements for the qualification of the unitrust and for the Donor's obtaining the full benefit of any income, gift and estate tax charitable deductions to which he (and his estate) may be entitled, section 664 of the Code, the regulations thereunder and the legislative and Treasury requirements shall govern.

IN WITNESS WHEREOF, the parties hereto have executed this Agreement the date first above written.

_____

John Doe, Donor

XYZ University
By:

_____

NOTES:

1. The percentage in paragraph 2(A) must be at least five percent (5%).

2. It is essential to omit the reference to "section 170(b)(1)(A)" if the remainderman is a private foundation or may be a private foundation at the time when any principal or income of the unitrust is to be distributed to it.

3. If the annual valuation date is not the first day of the taxable year, add:

> If the valuation date does not occur in a taxable year of the unitrust, other than the year in which the noncharitable interest terminates, the unitrust assets shall be valued as of the last day of that taxable year. In the taxable year in which the noncharitable interest terminates, if the valuation date does not occur before the day the noncharitable interest terminates, the unitrust assets shall be valued as of the day the noncharitable interest terminates.

4. If the annual valuation date is not the first day of the taxable year, substitute the following for the sentence reading, "The assets so added shall be valued at the time of contribution":

> Where no valuation date occurs after the time of the additional contribution and during the taxable year in which the additional contribution is made, the additional property shall be valued as of the time of the additional contribution.

Source: Northwestern University Estate Planning Advisory Council, Evanston, Illinois.

11

Conclusion

Let's summarize what we've learned about the CRT and those most likely to capitalize on its advantages.

The Tax Reform Act of 1969 created the Charitable Remainder Trust, an irrevocable tax-exempt trust available in annuity trust or unitrust formats. Properly structured, such trusts let the donor maintain control over all aspects of the trust, including the underlying investments, the amount and timing of income, and the organizations that will benefit from the charitable gift.

Some of the objectives a CRT can accomplish for a donor include:

- Establish a wealth accumulation account that grows free of current taxes, and has no limits on how much you can save and gives you a tax deduction.
- Own a tax-deductible, non-qualified private pension plan that grows free of current taxes, has no limits on

the amount of contributions, and provides you with a lifetime income.

- Avoid capital gains and estate taxation on the sale of highly appreciated assets like stocks, bonds, real estate, or even a business.
- Potentially increase inheritance to your family and heirs.
- Make a significant future charitable gift.

The two most popular types of the CRT are the Charitable Remainder Unitrust (CRUT) and the Charitable Remainder Annuity Trust (CRAT).

The CRUT pays a fixed percentage (at least 5%) of the value of the asset upon an annual valuation. Additional contributions are permitted. The income payout will fluctuate in direct proportion to the annual trust value.

There are three types of CRUTs:

- **Standard**, which pays out the fixed percentage of the annual trust value, regardless of the amount of trust income.
- **Net Income**, which pays out the fixed percentage of the annual trust value or annual income, whichever is less.
- **Net-Income-with-Make-Up (NIMCRUT)**, which pays out the fixed percentage of the annual trust value or annual income, whichever is less, and permits use of past income deficiencies in subsequent years when the trust earns more than the required payout.

The NIMCRUT offers the greatest flexibility when establishing a trust. As outlined in chapter six, significant benefits can be achieved by funding this type of trust with an annuity (as compared to other common investments).

The CRAT pays a fixed percentage (at least 5%) of the value of the assets on the date of transfer to the trust. Additional contributions to the trust are prohibited. The income payout remains constant regardless of the value of the trust asset or amount of trust income.

The fixed percentage of the CRUT or CRAT must be payable, at least annually, either for the life or lives of the income beneficiaries or for a term of years (not more than 20).

In chapters seven and eight, we examined the characteristics of what we called CRT prospects. Those with "charitable receptivity" either have some history of charitable giving or have specialized interests that might be channeled through the use of a CRT. Financial professionals should be advised that potential donors are not always aware of their own "charitable receptivity" and how it could be applied to enhance their own financial outlook.

As the theories of Earnest Becker suggest, it is simply a human trait to strive for some aspect of immortality. Often, this "immortality-striving," as he called it, is directly tied to our mortal motivations to make a difference, leave a legacy. The act of leaving something behind — usually a financial reward — to surviving family, charitable organizations, or both, accomplishes a level of achieving that immortality.

Because this characteristic is most apparent to us later in life, individuals in their retirement years or approaching retirement years are among the best prospects for a CRT. But, as we learned, there are many others whose financial situations present a golden opportunity to make the most of a CRT:

- Those planning for the future support of a spouse or loved one.
- Those looking to reduce taxes in real estate, income or other assets.

- Those with children approaching college age in need of additional income to cover tuition costs.
- Those who wish to leave wealth with a specific charitable organization(s) rather than for government distribution.
- Those looking to maximize wealth potential of a highly appreciated asset.

As we pointed out in chapter nine, it is important for potential donors and/or their financial advisors to do their homework on a charitable organization before bestowing that organization with a gift. Be sure the organization meets the tax-exempt criteria that meet your own financial objectives, then find out where and how your gift will be spent. Find out what percentage of the organization's income goes to the actual cause as opposed to fund-raising initiatives and administrative costs.

In marketing the CRT to potential donors, be sure to outline its advantages in detail while stressing the team approach to some of its more complex procedures.

Get started by contacting professionals with whom you are familiar to form that "CRT Team":

- An attorney for legal consultation and completion of the trust documents
- A certified public accountant (CPA) to review the income and tax benefits and complete the necessary filings
- A trust officer for the administration required after the trust is established
- A planned giving specialist

In seeking out potential donors, use the resources you already possess as a financial professional:

1. *Contact centers of influence.*
   Attorneys, CPAs, business brokers, trust officers, realtors. These are all good places to start. Ask them who they know who would fit the CRT "Donor Profile."
2. *Review your donor base.*
   Which donors do you have who fit the "Donor Profile"? Do you know of any donors who are involved with any charities, a church, university or college, etc.?
3. *Niche public seminars.*
   Once the audience has been tapped, the "CRT Team" can present easy and effective CRT seminars geared to donors and prospects.

Use this book to serve as a reference guide to learn the ins and outs of the CRT process and how to best spread the word about this unique giving technique.

The Charitable Remainder Trust has the potential to change the face of charitable giving in this country, from a concept of feeling good about giving, to a reality of doing well by doing good.